*Fashioning*
*Femininity*
*and English*
*Renaissance*
*Drama*

WOMEN IN CULTURE AND SOCIETY

*A series edited by Catharine R. Stimpson*

KAREN NEWMAN

# Fashioning Femininity and English Renaissance Drama

THE UNIVERSITY OF CHICAGO PRESS

*Chicago & London*

*Karen Newman* is professor of comparative literature and English at Brown University.

The University of Chicago Press, Chicago 60637
The University of Chicago Press, Ltd., London
©1991 by the University of Chicago
All rights reserved. Published 1991
Printed in the United States of America
00 99 98 97 96 95 94 93 92 91   5 4 3 2 1

Library of Congress Catalogue-in-Publication Data
Newman, Karen
  Fashioning femininity and English Renaissance drama / Karen
  Newman
    p. cm. — (Women in culture and society)
  Includes biographical references and index
  ISBN 0-226-57708-2 (cloth). —ISBN 0-226-57709-0 (paper)
  1. English drama—Early modern and Elizabethan, 1500-1600—History
  and criticism.   2. Women and literature—England—History—16th
  century.   3. Women and literature—England—History—17th century.
  4. English drama—17th century—History and criticism.
  5. Femininity (Psychology) in literature.   6. Sex role in
  literature.   I. Title.   II. Series.
  PR658.W6N48 1991
  822'.309352042—dc20                                        90-23374
                                                             CIP

Chapter 3 (originally titled "Renaissance Family Politics and Shakespeare's *The Taming of the Shrew*")is reproduced by permission from *English Literary Renaissance* 16 (1986): 86–100. Chapter 8 (originally titled "City Talk: Women and Commodification in Jonson's *Epicoene*") is reproduced by permission from *English Literary Renaissance* 53 (1989): 503–18.

*For Naomi*

*il n'y a que des contextes.*

Derrida,
"Signature Evénement Contexte"


*Le sol de nos sécurités bouge à mesure que se dévoile*
*le fait de ne plus pouvoir penser*
*une pensée d'hier.*

de Certeau,
*L'absent de l'histoire*

# CONTENTS

CONTENTS

# ILLUSTRATIONS

# SERIES EDITOR'S FOREWORD

*I*n the early 1590s, William Shakespeare wrote *The Taming of the Shrew*. Its leading characters—Kate, the shrew; Petruchio, the suitor who tames her—are among the most popular of literary couples. Indeed, at twelve, I played Kate in a much-abbreviated school version of the comedy. Six inches taller than my slight, crewcut, preadolescent Petruchio, I gargled out Kate's last words:

> . . . place your hands below your husband's foot;
> In token of which duty, if he please,
> My hand is ready, may it do him ease.
>      (V, ii, 177–79)

During the same decade of the Renaissance, a tragicomedy developed in Warwick, Shakespeare's home county. It was striking enough to enter English criminal law as an example of the dangers of circumstantial evidence.* Before his death, a man had appointed his brother to serve as the guardian of his daughter and land until she was sixteen. The uncle did his duty, teaching her both "book and needle," literacy and household skills. One day, when she was about eight or nine, he was disciplining her. She was heard to say, "Oh, good uncle, kill me not," and then she disappeared.

The uncle, who stood to inherit her property, was charged with murder and jailed, but released on bail in order to continue the search for the missing niece. Failing, he got another little girl to act as "the true child" at the next assizes. Discovered, his scam was taken as another indication of his guilt. He was hanged. A few years later, the "true child," now sixteen, showed up. Her story: the morning after her uncle had beaten her, she had run away. Comparatively well educated,

---

* I take the case and all quotations from J.W. Cecil Turner and A. LL. Armitage, *Cases on Criminal Law* (Cambridge: CambridgeUniversity Press, 1953), p. 437.

no doubt appealing, she had found "a stranger" in the next county to care for her until she came of age and could return to claim her land.

I juxtapose Shakespeare and the trial in his home county for two reasons. First, among other things, they dramatize gender relations in early modern England (1580–1640), the authority of men and its limits, the responses of women and girls to this authority and their limits. Gender relations are the starting point for the intellectual adventure of *Fashioning Femininity and English Renaissance Drama,* a deep, supple, graceful marvel of a book.

Early modern England was the site of great demographic, economic, political, and cultural changes, processes that help to constitute "the modern." These changes were as inseparable from gender as the rushing waters of a river are from their banks and bed. Inexorably, change bred anxiety about loss and loss of control. This attached itself to gender and stories about gender, a pattern that modernizing society after modernizing society repeats.

Inexorably, gender relations themselves mutated. Newman shows the construction of a different "femininity," a "female subject" that was body, a natural being, and wife, a familial being. She lived out a doubleness that a pun in the word "subject" conveys: to have an independent existence and yet to be submissive to a man, subject to his will, daughter to father, niece to uncle, wife to husband. A rhetorical reliance on binary oppositions easily polarized "male" and "female" and then ranked "male" more highly.

This hierarchy, however, was unstable, as is every sexual identity, every gender identity. Like the little girl in the Warwick assizes pretending to be the "true child," our sexual and gender identities are special kinds of fictions. We fashion them with a language, at a moment, in a milieu. We then call them immutable, as grievous an error as conflating the fabric of a sock with the foot it covers, the shod foot with the psyche. Women, moreover, resisted their subordinate roles, despite the punishments for such actions. Newman is alert to the appearance of "an oppositional femininity," especially in language, be it the ironic, bravura speech of Shakespeare's Kate or the scaffold confession of a Mother Waterhouse, about to be executed as a witch.

Crucially, gender and other sets of social relations influenced each other. Because of class, men were also the subjects of other men—

lords, masters, princes, rulers of an expanding state. This expanding state was becoming an empire. It had to confront and master the different, a task for travel literature. Newman looks at various sites of difference, from such colonial expansion to the extravaganzas of modern fashion. Among the most radical differences between the English and their Others were those of race. A contribution to the study of racism, Newman's chapter on *Othello* explores the marriage of Othello, the black man and racial Other, to Desdemona, the white woman and sexual Other, linked in love, death, and an ascribed, inscribed monstrosity.

I wrote that I began by juxtaposing *The Taming of the Shrew* and the story of a trial for two reasons. The second is this. *Fashioning Femininity* is also a bold, elegant example of a way of reading, writing, and naming history. Like the new historicists, Newman refuses to reduce history to "content," naked events, quantifiable trends, and paraphrasable themes. "History" is also the verbal, visual, and aural representation of events, the structures that articulate and give meaning to themes, the frames that organize reality—in brief, a discourse.

Such a vision of history calls for a merger of the interests of history, anthropology, art history, and rhetoric. Responding to that call, the literary critic and historian will extend her or his definition of "the textual" beyond "literature." The textual includes *The Taming of the Shrew* and a story from the Warwick assizes. Newman's title promises a study of English Renaissance drama, but she defines drama as an organized public spectacle, a representation staged for an audience to see. She is acutely sensitive to village rituals and Ben Jonson, a witch on trial and the witches in *Macbeth*.

Newman writes as well, "We need a different kind of textual intercourse, a promiscuous conversation of many texts, early modern elite and non-elite, historical records and ideological discourses, contemporary theory and popular culture" (p. 144). Faithful to her own perception, she satisfies this need by juxtaposing a number of theories against each other. Her range and clarity refute fretful, muddled accusations that theoreticians dismiss the materiality of history, disdain aesthetics, grouchily collapse culture and politics, and write obscurely.

From Derrida, Newman takes insights into difference, the boundlessness of context, and the operations of our restless signifiers; from

Marxism, an analysis of some relationships among production, ideology, and subjectivity; from psychoanalysis, a notion of the mother's centrality in the formation of gender; from feminist theory, a grasp of sexual difference, gender, and power. Together, these theories are neither a static synthesis that will serve as a fully explanatory map of reality, nor, alternatively, a friable collage that never will pan out. Rather, they are engaging elements in a multilogue in which we test ideas, probe for their flaws (a prime example is the ahistoricity of psychoanalysis), grapple for their strengths. We also put our own categories "into play." We suspect the hardness and solidity of "the literary," "the historical," "gender," or "woman," those nouns that grow high in our semantic fields, substantives that we abuse by confusing them with essences, substances.

I read *Fashioning Femininity* in amazement—delighted by its intelligence; delighted and appalled by the untameability of language, the untameability of the materials we ask language to tame, and the knottiness of the concurrent trials of acting, signifying, knowing, judging, feeling. I hope *Fashioning Femininity* will speak for itself to a large and equally delighted audience.

*Catharine R. Stimpson*

# ACKNOWLEDGMENTS

*R*ecent debates in Renaissance studies and feminist literary theory have posed what has seemed to me a false opposition between new historicism and feminist criticism. As my title publicly avows, with its allusion to Stephen Greenblatt's *Renaissance Self-Fashioning*, this book is "new historicist" in its preoccupation with subjects and their histories—with stories—and so owes a general debt to the work of Greenblatt, Louis Montrose, Steven Mullaney, and Stephen Orgel; but in its focus on gender, and more particularly its turn away from monarchs, it is in some ways closer to new historicism's older if brasher British counterpart, cultural materialism, and the work of Catherine Belsey, Jonathan Dollimore, Lisa Jardine, Alan Sinfield, and Peter Stallybrass. Finally it depends on the research of many social historians of early modern England, especially that of Susan Amussen, David Underdown, and Keith Wrightson.

The "femininity" of my title moves in different directions and is meant to acknowledge other intellectual relations—to feminist theory, poststructuralism, and psychoanalysis. Here my debts are at once more general and more specific: more general in that this book was prompted by my reading of what has come to be called "theory"; more specific because my encounters with theory have been mediated by friendships and all sorts of personal intellectual obligations: to Mary Ann Doane, Nancy Miller, and Nancy Vickers; to Margaret Ferguson for her exacting yet always generous reading of the entire manuscript; to Jonathan Goldberg, whose work wrestling with theory and history has continually challenged and provoked mine; and most especially as the dedication of this book witnesses, to Naomi Schor, sorely missed friend and colleague, who long ago goaded me to start this project by writing what now stands as the third chapter.

I have also benefited from many audiences, readers, and conversations that have, as convention has it, saved me from error and exaggeration; but special thanks go to members of an unnamed feminist reading group at Brown: Mary Ann Doane, Christina Crosby, Ellen Rooney, and Naomi Schor; to Stephen Foley, John Murchek, Elizabeth Weed, Remo Ceserani, Anita Piemonti; to the Pembroke Center Seminar 1987–88; and to the "Renaissance Seminar" at Wesleyan University. Thanks go to Nicole Cunningham for being a vigilant proofreader and a help in more ways than I can count. I am also grateful to the American Association of University Women and the Folger Shakespeare Library for support in the initial stages of my research and to the John Simon Guggenheim Memorial Foundation for the fellowship that enabled me to finish writing this book and get started on the next. More personal debts need no acknowledgment here.

*Bologna*
*May 1990*

# INTRODUCTION

S ed quis custodiet ipsos custodes?" Juvenal sardonically asks in his sixth satire: literally, "but who will guard the guardians themselves?" Though the line refers to the bodyguards whom Roman husbands hired to keep their wives faithful, it has been most often quoted in the context of political life to ask who will "insure the honesty of those entrusted with the public interest." So begins the "Tower Report," for example, the official account of the Iran-Contra affair.[1] Juvenal's misogynistic satire has become ungendered moral aphorism, his poetic line appropriated as cultural capital; women's supposed adulterous propensities, which drive them to illicit sexual behavior with hired watchdogs, stand in for the ethical and judicial failures of elected officials. This book records the slippage, illustrated in this commonplace appropriation of Juvenal's line, from femininity to politics, the ways in which gender is used, or alternatively, effaced, in the service of so-called larger political interests.[2] What is the relationship of gender to power and the state? How was femininity fashioned and deployed in early modern England?

Historians generally agree that between 1580 and 1640 England experienced enormous economic and demographic as well as political changes: a developing capitalist economy characterized by the growth and expansion of urban centers, particularly London; the rise of banking and overseas trade; and an increase in manufacturing with its concomitant need for credit and large amounts of capital. Urban development brought about a breakdown of community wherein effective means of social control such as compact, nucleated village centers, resident squires, and strong manorial institutions weakened or disappeared. High levels of inflation and unemployment led to an extraordinarily high turn-over in population among the poor, the middling sort, and even the gentry.[3]

Such changes were figured variously in the social fabric as acute anxiety about conventional hierarchies. Traditionally subject groups—merchants and actors, servants and apprentices—were enabled by such rapid social change to enter spheres of action customarily closed to them. Their entry and subsequent behavior, or even perhaps merely the spaces opened for them, threatened perceived hierarchies in Tudor and Stuart England. Though historians have argued convincingly that Renaissance women did not benefit from such changes, nevertheless men complained not only of upstart courtiership, a socially mobile middle class, and "masterless men," but of female rebellion. Incidents of feminine transgression crowd the historical record, and early printed books record and codify gender specific anxiety about changing social relations. As David Underdown has observed:

> Women scolding and brawling with their neighbors, single
> women refusing to enter service, wives dominating or even beat-
> ing their husbands: all seem to surface more frequently than in
> the periods immediately before or afterwards. It will not go un-
> noticed that this is also the period during which witchcraft accu-
> sations reach their peak.[4]

I begin from the assumption that, regardless of whether or not women had a Renaissance, as Joan Kelly has phrased it, gender was a significant way of *figuring* social relations in early modern England.[5]

In what follows, I focus in large measure on female subjectivity in both senses the expression allows—the construction of the gendered subject and the ideology of women's submission or subjection to men—though I recognize that both the theoretical and methodological assumptions of my work in part disallow that focus. Since identity, sexual difference, and even sexuality itself are fictions, constructed rather than "natural," not only the category "woman" but even "women" is problematic.[6] The focus on "women" risks perpetuating those categories by recirculating the very fictions about femininity and subjectivity this study aims to expose by reinscribing traditional notions of sexual difference grounded in essentialist epistemologies. Paradoxically, criticism that takes "women" as a governing category often disempowers women by representing them as victims of patriarchal domination. More importantly, such readings generally assume that, for example, the prescriptions for female behavior in a sermon or conduct book reflect women's lived experience, which the critic can decipher to provide a true account of Renaissance women's lives. Rarely are the problematic notions about language, reference, and truth employed in such readings questioned. Finally, in the early modern period, men were, after all, also subjects—to fathers, to masters, to lords, to their Prince—and their subjectivity was also constructed through proliferating discourses that share a great deal with the discourses of femininity I will be considering. The poststructuralist turn disallows any analysis of power and sexual politics in terms of easy binary divisions between oppressor and oppressed, dominant and subversive, male and female.

Despite these drawbacks, however, contemporary feminists' focus on "women" has had, and continues to have, enormous strategic importance: feminist work has almost single-handedly constructed gender as a category of analysis in critical discourse and thereby enabled different meanings and questions to be asked not only about gender but about power, subjectivity, and discourse itself. Furthermore, the focus on women has produced important effects of power, including the reformulation of disciplinary canons through the editing and publication of women's cultural productions.

Keeping in mind these objections, but also the instrumentality of the focus on women, I explore how the feminine subject is constructed by looking at representations of women on stage and in proliferating printed materials aimed at them. But I move increasingly away from "women" to ask instead how the category "femininity" is produced and deployed in early modern England. I attempt to analyze gender in terms of its local and specific formations rather than in terms of transhistorical categories to demonstrate how proliferating meanings in the discourses of femininity resist pat claims about patriarchal power and women's subject status. I hope at once to dislocate the hegemonic status of "patriarchy" in feminist readings of Renaissance texts *and* to show how gender has sometimes been displaced in new historicist readings preoccupied with the politics of colonialism, monarchy, and the elite. My perspective on gender will be multiple, intersected by perspectives of race, sexuality, and what we now term class.[7] What follows, then, is partial; located in particular debates within Renaissance studies, cultural studies, and feminist theory; and written and published over the past five years, during which the terms of literary and cultural analysis have changed rapidly.

In the first two chapters, I read a variety of texts—anatomies, conduct and domestic handbooks, sermons, homilies, ballads, catechisms, court cases—to delineate the ideologies of femininity they represented and produced. In the chapters that follow, I turn to a series of plays, which I read alongside various other historical documents, to show how female subjectivity was fashioned and represented in the urban culture of late sixteenth and early seventeenth century London. I focus on drama not merely because of the accidents of my own training and interests but because I argue that drama, as spectacle, provided a peculiarly useful locus for analyzing the production and management of femininity in early modern England.

# Body Politics

*that these masterly dames would but*
*glasse themselves*
   Snawsel, Looking glasse for married folkes

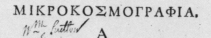

ΜΙΚΡΟΚΟΣΜΟΓΡΑΦΙΑ.

# A DESCRIPTION
## of the Body of Man.

TOGETHER
## VVITH THE CONTROVERSIES
### and Figures thereto belonging.

*Collected and Tranſlated out of all the Beſt Authors of Anatomy, Eſpecially
out of Gaſper Bauhinus, and Andreas Laurentius.* By HELKIAH CROOKE *Doctor in
Phyſicke, Phiſitian to His Maieſty, and His Hignesse* PROFESSOR *in Anatomy and Chirurgery.*

Publiſhed by the Kings Maieſties eſpeciall Direction and Warrant, according to the firſt
integrity, as it was Originally written by the AVTHOR.

—— *Etiam Parnaſſia Laurus*
*Parua, ſub ingenti matris ſe ſubijcit vmbra.*

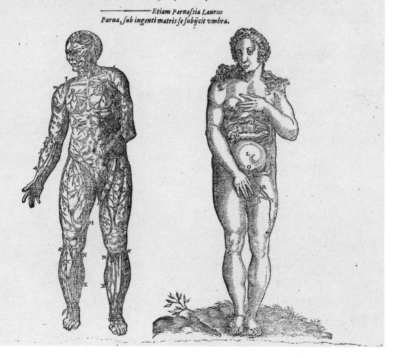

FIGURE ONE  Helkiah Crooke, *Microcosmographia, A Description of the Body
of Man*, title page (1615). By permission of the Folger Shakespeare Library.

$A$ s a child growing up in Dallas, Texas, I often visited the Museum of Health and Science to see the most entrancing exhibit, known locally as "the plastic man." We would enter the half-lit auditorium to sit in rows before a small stage flanked by plaster corinthian columns, in rapt attention, waiting for the show to begin. The lights would go down, music would play, curtains would open magically, and a gigantic plexiglass body would move forward on a rotating dais. A cultivated male voice would explain anatomy: all the arteries were red, the veins blue, and lights would illumine each organ as the voice from above named it. From this male model, schoolchildren on field trips or outings with their parents learned about the body. I always wondered why there was no plastic woman as well. When I returned to the museum as an adult with my young daughter, we found a matching female figure on its own rotating dais, identical to her companion except for her breasts and an odd detail: unlike her male counterpart, she had molded plastic hair.

On the title page of Helkiah Crooke's popular anatomy, *Microcosmographia, A Description of the Body of Man* (1615) (fig. 1), two bodies, male and female, stand side by side, both opened to the beholder's eye. Their *disposition* on the page, however, is remarkably different. The male figure stands alone, in air, flayed and fully exposed, frontally oriented, one foot forward as if in arrested movement. One hand is extended in a gesture of openness, the other casually out of the way behind his back. Lacking genitals, he displays the brain, the arteries, veins, and musculature of the unsexed body, of a sexually undifferentiated "Man." In contrast, the female figure is first and foremost a sexed body. She is represented in gestural modesty, with demurely flowing locks, one hand folded across her chest to hide her breasts, the other covering her genitals. Her lower torso is open to expose viscera, particularly her reproductive organs. Instead of floating in air like her male counterpart, the woman stands firmly on the ground in grass from which springs a leafy twig: she is of the earth, man apparently above it.

In Crooke's Anatomy, men and women both have bodies, but the woman's body is sexed, earthbound, mortal, of nature.[1] The iconographic model for Crooke's title page is the Genesis story, as figures 2 and 3 illustrate, but here the disposition of male and female signals a

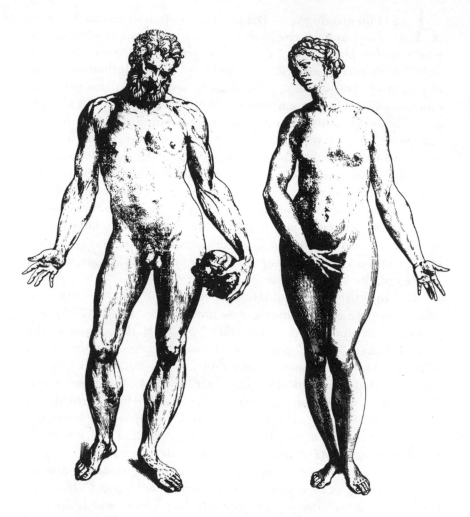

FIGURE TWO Andreas Vesalius, *Humani corporis fabrica librorum, Epitome*, K verso and L recto (1542). By permission of the University of Bologna.

temporal disjunction: man seems to be represented before the fall, in his glory, woman after the fall, in her shame. Crooke's Anatomy, written to illustrate the body biologically, represents social behavior: even anatomy codes the profoundly constructed character of sexual difference. In the early modern period, the female body is the site of dis-

FIGURE THREE Thomas Geminus, after Vesalius, *Compendiosa totius anatomie delineatio* (1545), interleaved between Bii verso and Biii recto. By courtesy of the Library of Congress.

courses that manage women: by continually working out sexual difference on and through the body, the social is presented as natural and therefore unchangeable, substantiated, filled with presence. Not only in anatomies and medical books but in other ideological texts, from

BODY POLITICS

sermons and homilies to broadsides and ballads, as well as in the social world of Elizabethan and Jacobean towns and villages available through the texts that give us access to that world, women were managed through their bodies.

But the speakers of those texts are almost invariably men; the male voice instructs (from *struere,* to build) femininity.[2] In early modern England, the anxiety generated by the unsubstantiated voice of God and the corruptible, fragile body of man is worked out not through the opposition of the human and divine but through sexual difference, through the woman's body and the man's voice, which—with the advent of printing and the growth of literacy, in part a response to the Reformation emphasis on the private study of scripture—is textualized and empowered in the act of reading.

In early modern England, man figures God's voice, representing his power, instantiating it, inscribing it, on woman's body; woman figures the human body, its corruptibility, fragility, but also its power to inspire desire, to multiply and reproduce. The female body is suspended in a political field in which all kinds of texts inscribe the spaces it can occupy (home, church, childbed, sickbed); the work it can perform (reproductive and household labor, charity work); how it is coded or marked as female (clothes, cosmetics, jewelry); the sounds and gestures it can appropriately emit; how it is punished for transgressing such codes; even how it is perceived and described (as a failed male body, as lacking in heat, as the pathetic obverse of the male, as a voracious mouth). How woman's body is invested with significance is determined in part by how it is utilized politically and economically, to reproduce not only biologically but socially as well, to reproduce fit subjects for church and commonwealth whose lineage is assured by chaste marriage. In the age of mechanical reproduction, the printed book disseminated ideologies of femininity to an unprecedentedly broad audience.

David Cressy claims only about 11 percent of Englishwomen were literate, a proportion that classes them below the lowest male category, labourers.[3] Cressy's statistics have been challenged on a number of grounds. Some historians question his criterion, the mark versus the signature.[4] Others point to the remarkable proliferation of pamphlets, ballads, and almanacs that suggest a larger non-elite reading public than Cressy's figures allow. Still others have shown through research on early English pedagogy that reading preceded writing in the curriculum, particularly for girls; in other words, more people may have had rudimentary reading skills than Cressy admits.[5] Certainly the proliferation of printed books in the vernacular addressed to women or a mixed audience during the late sixteenth and early seventeenth centuries implies a population at least willing to buy them if not able to read them.

But the discourses about femininity I am analyzing were disseminated in many ways other than the printed book read alone in a lady's closet—the eighteenth- and nineteenth-century middle-class model of the woman reader. Margaret Spufford admirably describes the early modern alternative: "Illiteracy was everywhere face to face with literacy, and the oral with the printed word" (32). Ideologies of femininity that shaped female subjectivity were disseminated on the liminal edges of literacy: in sermons preached from the pulpit and puritan scenes of communal reading, in exhortations urged from the magistrate's bench, in plays and popular pastimes, and in morning and evening prayers at home. Books devoted to female behavior and conduct were often addressed to women but with the explicit direction that the male reader would impart their wisdom to his silently attentive wife. In other words, ideologies of femininity were much more widespread than simple literacy percentages would suggest, though certainly the social status of the audience to which these materials were aimed was primarily the elite and "the middling sort," as historians have dubbed it—mostly urban and at least minimally educated.

In 1623 the Protestant preacher Thomas Gataker published "A Wife Indeed" in a volume entitled *Two Marriage Sermons*. In the dedicatory letter, Gataker claims to have preached the sermon at the marriage of Sir Robert Harlie to Ladie Brilliana so that the aptly named bride might "Therein, as in a Glasse, as you, Worthy Madam, may (I doubt not) see your selfe lively deciphered"; the inverted syntax and multiple parenthetical elements suggest perhaps more doubt than Gataker intends.[6] The link between women and the mirror is, of course, an ancient commonplace, part of a complex articulation of women as objects of male desire and dependent on that desire for their status, livelihood, even their lives. Derided for her narcissism and

*Lavinia as memento mori.*

preoccupation with the material, the woman before a mirror epitomizes the memento mori. Attached to the beauty of her reflection,
with a figure of death looking over her shoulder, the woman at her
glass figures mutability and the transience of the body in contemporary paintings, emblems, and engravings.

Beside this long tradition is another, rival tradition derived from
an ancient topos found in Plutarch, perhaps the most common Renaissance source. There the metaphor of the glass is a site of ethical exempla. The lives of ancient heros and their traces in texts, as in the case
of Plutarch, were mirrors wherein readers could learn proper forms of
behavior or lessons about improper forms. Perhaps the most widely
known example in Renaissance England is the *Mirror for Magistrates*. In
the early modern period, these two problematics of the mirror come
together in the management of women. The ideological texts written
to advise women how to behave continually allude to the mirror, often
in their titles: there were glasses for ladies and for drunkards, glasses
of marriage and of health. Women were continually exhorted by
speakers to "glass" themselves as Gataker does Lady Brilliana. Sir Robert himself is exhorted differently; he is to learn "what a pretious
Jewell God hath in her bestowed."[7] Gataker's figure to Sir Robert is
one of possession and objectification, the ubiquitous feminine inverse
of personification. His wife is a jewel bestowed by God, though God's
gift of a wife does not prevent Gataker from detailing at length the
procedures for choosing a good one.

The following sermon is a series of glosses on Proverbs that details
the duties of a wife. As his title suggests, Gataker is anxious about the
relationship between signifier and referent, words and things or actions: what, he asks, is a wife in *deed*?

> But the *Woman* that beareth the *Name,* and standeth in the *roome*
> of *a Wife,* but doth not the *office* and *dutie* of *a Wife,* is but as *an*
> *eye of glasse,* or *a silver nose,* or *an ivorie tooth,* or *an iron hand,* or *a*
> *wooden leg,* that occupieth the *place* indeed, and beareth the *Name*
> of *a limbe* or *a member,* but is not truly or properly any *part* of that
> *bodie* wherenunto it is fastned; it is but *equivocally* so called. (Fi[r])

*false*
*synecdoche*

Gataker's sermon resembles numerous contemporary examples:
it conforms to the conventions of the marriage sermon predictably,

but his extended metaphor for describing what a woman is if she "doth not the *office* and *dutie* of *a Wife*" deserves close attention. In his inverted *blason,* woman is a series of prosthetic parts and the "*bodie* whereunto it is fastned" is the husband. The larger metaphorical frame is the Pauline letter to the Ephesians, the commonplace notion of marriage as the union of man and woman into one flesh, but Gataker's male body is strangely ravaged by disease, and the disease would seem to be syphilis.

The woman who fails to conform to her wifely duty—subjection, obedience, silence, chastity, as the handbooks present it—is metonymized as a series of members "fastned" to her husband's body.[8] "Fasten" plays on the commonplace Renaissance term for the marriage contract or vow, "handfasting." Significantly, these false members are all of great value and workmanship, and are made from materials signaling the very geographical explorations that brought the pock to the old world: ivory, silver, hardwood. Gataker's metaphor implicitly suggests that a woman who is not a wife indeed is to blame for her husband's adulteries and their effects, here the syphilitic body.

In many of these texts, women are not urged merely to chastity, obedience, and silence; they are admonished to repress even gestures and facial expressions, *any visual sign* of opposition to their husbands: "the eye and the speach are the mindes Glasses.[9]" In Becon's *Catechisme* women are to obey "with the head, eies, tong, lippes, hands, feete, or with any other parts of the body," or as another writer puts it, the "parts of her body, the eye, the brow, the nostrils, the hands, the feete, the shoulders, [must] be kept in so good order," and the wife "should resolve never to breake forth into such exorbitant carriage as may justly challenge blowes."[10] In the early seventeenth-century treatise *Counsel to the Husband: to the Wife Instruction* (1608), women are exhorted even in the face of male tyranny, drunkenness, and abuse, not to fret, scold, or scowl, for "if such saw their faces then in a glasse, it would make them love the practise of such behaviour the worse for ever" (E5$^r$).

To "B. S.," the aptly initialed author of this little treatise, and to most of his contemporaries, even as they sometimes exhort men not to be tyrants in their exaction of obedience from their wives, they claim "the cause of contention may be in the husband, but the fault of contenting, is surely in the wife" (E6ᵛ). The Protestant divine William Whately exhorts women to keep silence and men not to beat their wives, claiming that for the husband to do so is "to make an incision into his own flesh" (Zʳ). But he quickly withdraws this critique of male behavior, often quoted as evidence of a changed attitude toward women to argue that physical violence is necessary when "grosse and exorbitant sinnes" are persisted in, and continuing the metaphor of the husband as surgeon, claims such abuse is like cauterizing with a hot iron, and should be performed "as if he were faine to strike his owne heart, with demonstration of much backwardnes, loathnes & unwillingnes, & with such a grieved countenance, sorrowfull behaviour and lamenting words" (Z2ᵛ). The representation of the husband as teacher, master, healing surgeon, runs throughout these texts, a means of glorifying male endeavor, privilege, power, even sadism, and justifying female submission. Though such discussions might demonstrate a new attitude toward women by showing that wife-beating is no longer unremarkable, they also represent, by bringing into discourse the husband's power over his wife's body, an obsessive, even self-conscious *display* of masculine agency.

These descriptions of gestural obedience are part of a rhetorical disciplining of the female body by fragmenting it, most emphatically perhaps in the *blason*. Anatomization was a strategy for managing femininity and controlling its uses, not only in love poetry or the wedding sermon but in the drama as well. Women frequently were figured synecdochically, as mouths, gaping and voracious. A striking example is found in Thomas Becon's *Catechisme* (1564) in which he inveighs against adulterous women and their voracious sexuality: "The whore is never satisfied, but is like as one that goeth by the way & is thirstye: even so does she open her mouth, and drinke of everye next water, that she may get. By every hedge she sits down, & opēs her quiver against every arow. The godly maried woman cannot be entised neither with faire words nor with gifts to defile her husbands bed."[11] Here woman's presumed closer intimacy with nature and her rampant sexuality are enacted metaphorically by making her genitals a thirsty mouth roaming the countryside in search of water. The mixed metaphor, from mouth/water to quiver/arrow to gift/exchange signals not only a violent misogyny but exchange value and even perhaps covert desire. Man, by contrast, is linked to cultural signs rather than nature; he solicits intercourse with words and gifts and possesses the marital bed rather than taking pleasure "by every hedge."

The fragmentation of the female body into parts, and particularly the obsession with the female mouth, is not always focused literally on the genitals only but on the mouth as source of speech as well, as we see in the shift from Becon's focus on sexuality to the Protestant preacher Henry Smith's focus on silence. In describing how to choose a good wife, Smith exhorts his presumed male reader to look for signs of fitness: godliness, a modest look, and modest speech, "or rather her silence, for the ornamēt of a woman is silence. . . As the open vessels were counted uncleane; so account that the open mouth hath much uncleannes."[12] Here women's two mouths are conflated; disallowed speech is a sign throughout the period of sexual transgression. So in the public rituals enacted against scolds and shrews and those against adulteresses, both forms of behavior were punished similarly—with skimmingtons or the charivari. An open mouth and immodest speech are tantamount to open genitals and immodest acts.

I want to return briefly to the title page from Crooke's anatomy (fig. 1). To read Crooke's two bodies according to hierarchized polarities—male/female, active/passive, culture/nature, pre-lapsarian/post-lapsarian—is to repress the instability of these images and the play of *différance* they produce that resists both the critical lament of the victim characteristic of some feminist work and the new historicist's resigned claims of "containment" as well.[13] An excess of signification proliferates meanings in unexpected directions, directions those very oppositions attempt to circumscribe but at which they never fully succeed. The neutral male body, however "normative" in its representation of arteries and veins and its openness and power, is also castrated, flayed of protective skin, hairless, traversed by intersecting lines that seemingly entrap it, its left arm oddly amputated, its right arm perhaps extended in supplication. The female body, represented as close to nature, modest, even ashamed, is overdetermined, polysemic. The image derives from the repertory of Italian Renaissance art, the conventional pose of a Venus *pudica*. As such, it is linked to culture, the made, and therefore troubles the culture/nature polarity the figures initially produce.

BODY POLITICS

The Latin quotation that appears above the two figures, "etiam Parnasia laurus/parva sub ingenti matris se subiicit umbra" (literally, "even the small Parnasian bay laurel shoots up beneath its parent's massive shade"),works in similar double fashion. It is taken from book II of the *Georgics* on the various ways trees are propogated. Virgil not only describes the habit of the bay tree but self-consciously alludes to his poetic art, which imitates his "parent" Hesiod. *Parnasia* refers, of course, to the mountain sacred to Apollo, god of poetry and medicine, whose temple at Delphi stood near Mount Parnassus. Crooke uses the lines to pay tribute punningly to his own predecessors, Gaspar Bauhinus and especially Andreas Laurentius (hence the pun on *laurus*), the "best authors" from whom he claims to have "collected and translated" his *Description of the Body of Man*. The Latin *matris* in the botanical context means "of parent stock," but in relation to the female figure below it, which looms above the small branch at its feet, *matris* suggests the more common meaning "mother." Figuratively, then, in conjunction with the visual image, the lines suggest the generative power of the female body, but here, instead of producing the "natural" human child, it is the book, Crooke's anatomy, that is born beneath its massive shade. Cultural production has supplanted natural generation.

The ideological discourses with which I began can also be mobilized to undermine those very hegemonic discourses. Ideology becomes an Imaginary, unfixed, phantasmagoric, at once enabling and at the same time oppressive.[14] Here, the conventional representation of sexual difference displays what it seems to exclude. The signifying power of the image contradicts the social coding of represented feminine modesty by emphasizing female sexuality, exposing it while seeming to hide it modestly. Similarly, the fragmentation of the female body I have analyzed in marriage sermons, conduct books, and the like not only masters by dismembering but also threatens such mastery through that very dispersion and the semiotic instabilities it sets in motion. In Gataker's sermon, the marital body is a hybrid, a cyborg in which colonial anxiety is displaced onto the failed wife whose body, far from being natural and organic, has become "commodities"—silver, hardwood, ivory.[15] Gataker's blason problematizes the notion of "body" itself.

CHAPTER ONE

# The Crown Conjugal: Marriage in Early Modern England

*A good wife is the crown of her husband,*
*but she who brings shame is like*
*rottenness in his bones.*
　　Proverbs 12:4

*T*he Protestant Reformation witnessed the triumph of God's word in print and made available to the literate scriptural models for human behavior and social organization.[1] Among the Protestant writers on marriage, continental and English, the Bible presented a series of texts for modeling and understanding the marital relation—most notably texts from Proverbs and the Pauline letters.[2] Marriage was justified against the Catholic ideal of celibacy: "He that finds a wife finds a good thing, and obtains favor from the Lord" (Proverbs 18:22). Proverbs was sometimes called the "Christian Mans Ethicks" and claimed as having preeminence above "most, if not all, the *Bookes* in the *Bible.*"[3] But the most widely cited scripture from Proverbs in the marriage handbooks, sermons, and the like, is the metaphor used as the epigraph of this chapter: "A good wife is the crown of her husband." This text and others like it provided a basis for a particular kind of synecdochic representation of woman that managed female behavior by disposing the female body in figures that self-consciously display masculine agency.

The Biblical verse from Proverbs represents woman metonymically as the crown of her husband. A crown is first an ornament for the head. Worn not simply for personal adornment, it is a mark of the wearer's honor or achievement. A good wife, then, is a mark of her husband's achievement, and the handbooks' emphasis on the role of the husband in educating and molding his wife to obedience, submission, and good housewifery witnesses such a view of that role. A crown is also a token worn by a monarch as a sign of sovereignty; thus the figure also sustains the patriarchal organization of the household in early modern England and the microcosm/macrocosm analogy on which it depends. In his *Crown Conjugall or the Spouse Royal* (1620), John Wing expresses this view with virtually epigrammatic force: "*Every Husband,* is his *Wives King;* though *every Wife* be not her Husbands crowne...we do not lose our pre-heminence, by your disobedience."[4] More often than not, the second half of the proverb, "she who brings shame is like rottenness in his bones," is missing from these texts, not so much because of a changed, more positive view of women and marriage as is sometimes claimed, but arguably as a form of management by erasure: the shameful wife is literally unrepresented, she is not written.

THE CROWN CONJUGAL

Another key Biblical text in writing on marriage is taken from Ephesians: "Wives, be subject to your husbands, as to the Lord. For the husband is the head of the wife as Christ is the head of the church, his body, and is himself its Savior. As the church is subject to Christ, so let wives also be subject in everything to their husbands" (6:22–25). This text is used to justify both marriage and the subjection of wives. In the subsequent exhortation to husbands, "Husbands, love your wives as Christ loved the church...husbands should love their wives as their own bodies" (6:25, 28) and throughout the writings on marriage, man is figured as the head, woman as the body; they are one flesh, a Renaissance commonplace. But this union is not equal in that the male term—head, mind, and by analogy here, Christ— has a positive value, while the female term has sometimes merely a lesser value, sometimes a more directly negative value. Women are bodies, associated with nature; and as the suppressed half of the verse from Proverbs demonstrates, bad wives are rottenness in the bones.

In early modern England, women were represented within the family and the roles it allowed, erotic or conjugal. The overdetermined relation between the family and society, between familial and political authority, with which power relations were represented in late Elizabethan and early Jacobean England made the family at once a site of contest and containment. As the basic unit of production as well as consumption, of the pooling and distribution of resources, and of the reproduction of fit subjects for the commonwealth, the family and woman's key role in it were widely recognized.[5] Managing femininity so as to insure the reproduction of the commonwealth, great and small, was a significant ideological feature of early modern England. Political allegiances were perceived in terms of familial duty and familial relations in terms of the body politic. The analogy between family and politics was so powerful that even Elizabeth's defender against John Knox's attack on women's rule felt compelled to excuse her authority by claiming "a woman may rule as a magistrate, yet obey as a wife."[6] Homilies, sermons, conduct books all rehearse the lesson put most emphatically in Alexander Nowell's *Catechism* (1563) "not only parents, but all those to whom any authority be given, as magistrates, ministers...are contained under the name of fathers."[7]

We must be careful, however, not to take the microcosm/macrocosm analogy literally, as preachers and political theorists of the early modern period did, and as many modern readers have; to do so is to commit the ontological phallacy that sees the father and the family as at the origins of social life and the polis. Patriarchalism justified absolutism juridically and constituted desire psychologically; but like femininity, it was a construct, not a given. The family was not, as Gentian Hervet translated Xenophon in 1532 (with at least seven editions before the end of the century), the "first society in nature, and the ground of all the rest." Fathers were not sovereigns, or even their representatives, and many of these texts on marriage and the family betray their recognition of that difference.

Despite their analogical claims of identity between the family and the commonwealth, contemporary writers themselves recognized the difference between woman's status in the family and the status of other subjects. They recognized the special nearness of wives, their knowledge of their husbands' habits and faults, and the possibility they might use that knowledge against them—in short, they recognized the circulation of power within the sexual relation and the threat of sexual difference. As the popular Puritan divine William Whately puts it in his *A Bride-Bush* (1623), "The wife is indeed an inferiour, but very neare and very familiar."[8] The continued rehearsal of the microcosm/macrocosm trope represents the construction of an enabling ideology for consolidating sovereign power in the state: masters of families were exhorted to join hands with magistrates to insure the orderly working of the commonwealth. During the early modern period, sexual difference was ordered within the framework of such tropes.

If the constant refrain of preachers and poets was the subjection of women—every conduct book, every marriage sermon begins by making this point—that refrain must be seen in terms of the general exhortations to subjection such as the "Homily on Obedience" that required submission of everyone, male and female, even of the rocks and stars.[9] Peter Laslett calls this phenomenon "subsumption" and claims that "all those in life cycle service, all women, all unmarried persons...were 'subsumed'...into the personalities of their fathers and masters."[10] But Laslett's generalization and the "Homily on Obedience" both obscure the destabilizing effects of status and degree on the ideology of subjection. In the daily life of household, village, and town, women, for example, though always ideologically subject, often had authority over men—over their servants and children, over the less wealthy or wellborn. Furthermore, feminine subjectivity was theorized even in the early modern period differently from other subject positions.

In his *A Golden Keye opening the Locke to Eternall Happiness*, (1609), Francis Dillingham distinguishes between the subjection of servants and of wives. A servant, he claims, is "servily subject" because he "worketh for another," but a wife is "politiquely subject" because she "worketh for [her] owne good."[11] A woman, then, is doubly a subject: subjected to her husband in obedience, according to God's ordinance in Genesis and thus modeling the relation of subject to sovereign, but also, and more importantly, constructed as a subject by a system of relations—textual, social, institutional—that fashioned her very subjectivity and the shape and kind of available perceptions of her. In using the term patriarchal, I do not claim that Elizabethan and Jacobean England was a patriarchal culture in the precise sense of a society ruled by fathers, but rather that patriarchalism was a dominant trope through which social relations were perceived, a strategy whereby power was embodied and institutionalized.

Precisely because relations within the family were insular and heterogeneous, because the relations between men and women within families were different from other sorts of social relations and less subject to other mechanisms of power, political philosophers, preachers, and magistrates alike sought to render them like by means of such comparisons. The microcosm/macrocosm analogy depends on the whole series of hierarchized binarisms often represented in sermons, handbooks, and homilies of the period, particularly in later puritan texts such as the Bishop of Salisbury's "A Wedding Sermon" (1608), in which he elaborates a whole series of binarisms and the duties appointed to each: Prince/subject, pastor/flock, husband/wife, parents/children, master/servant, rich/poor, high/low—all deemed ordained by God.

Some historians and literary critics have claimed that the Reformation promulgated new ideals of marriage based on love and companionship that bettered the status of women in early modern Europe.[12] Marriage handbooks, sermons, letters, and the like are marshaled to demonstrate a change from their Catholic counterparts that, as the argument goes, focused, or indeed obsessed on, woman's inferior status, her uncleanness, and on marriage as a last resort for those men unable to realize the ideal of chastity. Protestant writers are said to have redefined chastity to include chaste married love, to have put companionship above the need to avoid fornication, the traditional reason for marrying, and to have fostered a new level of affect in the marital relation. Even when the evidence of parish registers, church court records, and folk customs is adduced to suggest that marital and familial attitudes and behaviors, among the poor and middling sort at least, remained remarkably consistent over time at least until the nineteenth century,[13] as Kathleen M. Davies observes: "The notion that these texts describe a new *ideal* of family relationships, whether that ideal was practised or not, has survived this criticism. A fairly standard list of writers tends to be quoted to support the view that there was a new ideal of mutuality in marriage, which was a direct outcome of Puritan theological principles."[14] But Davies argues convincingly that a review of early and late works, secular and religious, demonstrates remarkable continuity. Both continually reiterate the theme of women's subjection; Catholic, early reform, and Puritan works alike, following Augustine, brand pleasurable or passionate marital intercourse as adulterous.[15] Religious handbooks and sermons, as well as secular works, all represent sexual roles in binary terms: men love, women submit; men speak, women are silent; men provide through work outside the home, women are confined to the home. Davies concludes that the continuity in advice "about the purposes of marriage and about the relationship between husband and wife in all its behavioral aspects—choice of partner, dominance of husband, mutual affection and respect, sexual activity, and sharing of work—[ ] indicate that Puritan conduct books do not show any *change* to domesticity and affection as ideals of marriage. There was nothing new in such ideals."[16]

Though few of the early or later works are as adamant as the reform theologian Thomas Becon, who exhorts women to stay at home and avoid taverns, neighbors, and places where plays, interludes, and pastimes are held, emerging only for "urgent, weighty &

necessary causes" such as church, the illness of a neighbor, or the market, both Catholic and Reformation examples support Davies's conclusions.

But there are nevertheless important differences in *how* this marital advice is presented, and in the ways these texts represent and produce femininity. Instead of using the Reformation as a dividing line with a negative Catholic attitude toward marriage on one side, a changed post-Reformation ideal of mutuality on the other, we can discern gradual shifts in the means of fashioning femininity from the pre- and early Reformation period to the early seventeenth century up to the English Civil War, shifts that had important consequences for how women were interpellated, in Althusser's term, as subjects in early modern England.[17] The historians' attention only to content misses significant differences in the rhetorical organization of these texts, an organization that in the later Puritan works reinforced the binary oppositions on which descriptions of the family depended.

Catholic and early reform writers organize their texts according to the rhetorical principles and practices of *copia*: as Thomas Wilson puts it in his *Arte of Rhetorique* (1560), "he that mindeth to perswade, must needes be well stored with examples."[18] Writers used commonplace books and the *florilegia* to "stock" the imagination with "matter"—proverbs, idiomatic and epigrammatic expressions, allusions, apothegms, stock comparisons, conventional serial adjectives, "sentences," and *exempla*—to produce a heteroglossic richness different from later modes of composition.[19] That richness depends on the play of signifiers, on aural echoes, verbal associations, on a productive process of difference and deferral in which meanings proliferate on many cognitive axes— sensory, psychological, intellectual—on what Derrida has termed *différance*.

In these texts the feminine is unstable, powerfully productive even when it is negatively represented. Adultery and whoredom, for example, are common topics in the early texts and are presented as dangers to marriage.[20] In the Catholic William Harrington's *In this boke are conteyned the comendacions of matrymony* (1528), he expatiates on adultery, its widespread presence, its evil, its punishment, as does the early Lutheran treatise, Heinrich Bullinger's *The Christian State of Matrimony*, printed in English in 1541 (with seven editions by 1575). Bullinger's translator, Myles Coverdale, claims in his dedicatory letter to the Christian reader that his translation was prompted because "adultery is now become altogether common & shamelesse in the world." Bullinger is preoccupied with illicit sexuality; the centerpiece is a long diatribe against whoredom and adultery, three times the length of any other chapter, filled with every kind of example: how adultery is punished in other nations, even by pagans; how women are sexually voracious, dangerous and mercenary. In a brief dramatic dialogue inserted pell-mell into the middle of his tirade, Bullinger represents a whore saying to a naïve client: "no more money, no more love." The woman is denigrated for the mercenary use of her body and the man for his submission to her, but Bullinger betrays a grudging if derisive respect for the whore's mercantile good sense. From the whore's thrift, the text moves associatively to the good housewife's management of her household and a long list of proverbs on household thrift and administration. The text turns on an economy of thrift, psychological as well as fiscal, on "thrift" and its commonplaces, not on the opposition between whore and good wife. As the examples multiply, generated through a series of aural, mental, and figurative echoes, the reader loses control over Bullinger's praise and blame and is caught up in the equivocal meanings and heteroglossic voices produced by rhetorical amplification.

Between the early sixteenth-century works on the family and matrimony in which woman's place, duty, and "nature" figure prominently, and the later sermons and conduct books of the 1590s and early seventeenth century, a shift takes place in the mode of organizing writing, the shorthand term for which is "method." "Method" was the practice of classifying concepts by dichotomies: a subject was defined by division into halves, those halves into halves, and so on, down to so-called indivisibles or essentials. Subjects were divided into component parts, then subdivided, until indivisible arguments had all been enumerated. "Method" was a means of representing knowledge, but its practitioners believed it to be more than merely a clear and useful taxonomy: knowledge was produced by means of dichotomies; method was a means of discovering Truth.[21] By the late sixteenth century, "method" was the rage, the most popular means of educating generations of schoolboys; its vogue generated an enormous market for books proposing various "methods," "systems," and "analyses."[22]

"Method" changed the Renaissance and subsequent western intellectual tradition in that it naturalized the habits of thinking we have come to call western metaphysics. Walter Ong traces this shift to the dissemination and extraordinary popularity of Peter Ramus's *Dialecticae Libri Duo*: "Ramus' influence is in school or university textbooks, and is perpetuated as part of that great deposit of textbook literature dealing with the most familiar of our ideas which is rewritten in every generation, while remaining so much a part of the universal heritage that no one can believe it has ever changed or even derived from a particular source."[23] According to Ong, what was once Ramist logic seems always already there: it has cast "off Ramus' name and become simply logic" or "method." But to attribute the late sixteenth- and early seventeenth-century preoccupation with method to Ramus is to privilege the notion of "author" and what Foucault refers to as the "moment of *individualization* in the history of ideas." The domination of "method" was produced not by the work of an individual author, Ramus, but as the result of a variety of cultural interests, a concatenation of practices and conditions—scientific, pedagogic, linguistic, theological, philosophic, technological.

The point is not to reduce western metaphysics and the intellectual habit of binary thinking to Renaissance "method" or Ramism but rather to locate the historical specificity of one moment when such habits of mind were consolidated and codified. Ong describes the importance of "method" to the Renaissance with an apt metaphor. "Method," he claims,

> released enthusiasms such as that of Jean Bodin, who seeks to "methodize" man's understanding even of history, and prepared the way for the more gargantuan enthusiasms of the German systematic encyclopedists and thus indirectly for the still later French *Encyclopédistes*. Here it served somewhat as a crystal introduced into a supersaturated solution, suddenly precipitating and giving structure to the interest in method with which the scholastic world in Paris was charged. (297)

The Puritan divines who wrote conduct books and marriage sermons in the 1590s and early decades of the seventeenth century, men like William Gouge, William Whately, Dudley Fenner, and R. Abbot, lay out their ideas about marriage by "method"; that is, they organize their texts to produce "knowledge" by means of dichotomies or binary oppositions. As Gouge himself puts it in describing the duties of husband and wife in marriage, "because contraries laid together doe much set forth each other in their lively colours, I have to every duty annexed the contrary faults."[24]

Figure 4 illustrates the way in which "method" ordered sexual relations. Marriage and sexual difference are represented spatially, by means of tables that oppose man and woman, their duties, natures, behaviors and activities.[25] Susan Amussen claims that this binary organization represents an ideal of reciprocity and complementarity "in which obedience was given in return for care and protection" and relates it to contract theories of the state, which she contrasts with patriarchalism. But it is important to resist the tendency to claim the contract retrospectively as the operative dynamic of early modern marriage. Theoretically, the reciprocity of the contract is not a "solution" to the gender hierarchies of marriage and sexual relations but rather an important site of their production. The term "contract" obscures the discursive construction of gender binarisms since "the economy of binary opposition, [is] itself a ruse for a monologic elaboration of the masculine."[26]

The ideal of *copia,* more akin to a postmodernist aesthetic that values the elaboration of unsubordinated details over structure, does not erase the binary so much as collapse polarities by foregrounding each of the terms "as the *différance* of the other, as the other different and deferred in the economy of the same (the intelligible as differing-deferring the sensible, as the sensible different and deferred; the concept as different and deferred, differing-deferring intuition; culture as nature different and deferred, differing-deferring."[27] The whore and the housewife, linked alliteratively and associatively through a shared economy of thrift and the deployment of its places, produced knowledge as word, as the play of differences. The practice of method, with its taxonomy of dichotomized categories, changed the organization and material look of these texts: thinking about an idea meant subject-

# The Contents.

1. To the husband, which are
  - 1. To gouerne or rule, to which end he must
    - 1. Keepe his authoritie, whereof the meanes are
      - 1. Generally to liue well.
      - 2. Specially to shunne
        - 1. Bitternes.
        - 2. Vnthriftines.
        - 3. Lightnes.
      - Ch. 8.
    - 2. To vse his authoritie: for which end he must know three things.
      - 1. The parts of authoritie.
      - 2. The end of vsing it : } of which he is informed, Chap. 9.
      - 3. The manner of vsing it, by practising three vertues.
        - 1. Iustice, of which Chap. 10.
        - 2. Wisdom, of which Chap. 11.
        - 3. Mildnes, of which Chap. 12.
  - 2. To maintaine her, both whilest he liues with her, and by his Will at death, of which, Ch. 13.
2. To the Wife, which all come to two heads. viz.
  - 1. She must acknowledge her inferioritie.
  - 2. She must carry her selfe as inferiour.
    - 1. By shewing reuerence towards his person, both
      - 1. Inward in heart.
      - 2. Outward in
        - 1. Her speeches.
          - 1. To him.
          - 2. Before him to others.
          - 3. Of him behinde his backe.
        - 2. In her gestures, countenances, and whole behauiour.
      - of which Ch. 14.
    - 2. By practising the vertue of subiection to
      - 1. His directions, and that by obeying him both
        - 1. In all things.
        - 2. Willingly.
      - 2. Reproofes, and chasticements, and that by
        - 1. Receiuing such as are deserued, fruitfully.
        - 2. Bearing such as are vndeserued, patiently.

FIGURE FOUR William Whately, *A Bride-Bush*, A4 verso (1623).
By permission of the Folger Shakespeare Library.

ing it to "method," to polarized and hierarchized categories—here the sexual division of behavior and labor. Logically patriarchalism requires and produces an other: femininity, childhood, or servitude—wives, children or servants, whose obedience in the family figures the obedience of subjects to Prince. "Methodizing" discourse promoted rigid sexual divisions more prominently than earlier rhetorical forms based on *copia*.[28]

The importance of the binary figuration of social relations is increasingly apparent from the 1580s onward during the period of acute anxiety over the succession, in marriage handbooks and sermons that emphasize the microcosm/macrocosm analogy. By the 1590s and the early decades of the seventeenth century, with the publication of William Perkins' *Christian Oeconomie* (Lat. 1590, tr. 1609), the preoccupation with adultery and whoredom characteristic of the early conduct books, handbooks, and sermons virtually disappears. The traditional biblical origins of marriage, the analogy between the marriage of husband and wife and that of Christ and the church, and the conventional duties of husband and wife—he loves and provides, she submits and obeys—remain. But the elaborate attacks on adultery and whoredom are increasingly displaced by representations of ordered family life: in the words of Thomas Pickering, Perkins's translator, the family is a "seminary," a means of ordering the church and commonwealth; if the family fails, the commonwealth fails. This shifting figuration of the family is apparent not only in the religiously motivated handbooks and sermons by preachers, often dedicated to members of the peerage or gentry, but also in more popular works, such as Alexander Niccholes, *A Discourse of Marriage and Wiving* (1620) or Robert Snawsel's lively dialogue, *A Looking glasse for married folkes* (1610).

The shift away from the destructive power of female sexuality and adultery, toward the positive effect of a "good" marriage and well-ordered family on the social and political order, might at first seem to support the claims that puritan writing on marriage enhanced the status of marriage and therefore of women. But the later Protestant discourses on women and marriage represent less a change in the status of women or in attitudes toward them than, as I have argued, a change in how they are interpellated as social and sexual subjects. The emphasis on the duties and conduct of marriage represents a form of social regulation, as the explicit analogies between the family and the commonwealth witness, not a sentimental recognition of the importance of domestic affairs or heterosexual relations. Perhaps the most telling description of the wife's subject relation to her husband is found not, as might be expected, in an early text but in one of the often-quoted so-called companionate handbooks, William Whately's *A Bride-Bush* (1619). He exhorts women to obedience even in the face of a drunken, brawling husband, observing that: "it is not for a prisoner to breake prison at his pleasure, because he hath met with a rough jaylour" (Ee3ʳ).

*wow!*

The suppression of the discourse about whoredom and adultery, far from illustrating a new sense of women's worth and dignity, points to newly mobilizable means of managing and regulating sexual difference. In Catholic and early reform works, women's voracious sexuality is managed by means of public shaming and spectacle in elaborate descriptions of how adulteresses are punished, from Germany to Israel to Cathay, among the ancients and in the present day. Women suspected of or caught in adultery were publicly shamed: woman's body, constructed by religious doctrine as the "source" of sin, must pay its price. In Germany, for example, Bullinger describes how the husband "strippe [sic] her out of her clothes, thrust her out of his house, and beate her openly with rods in the citye or towne, even before her friends." In early English judicial records involving women who bear illegitimate children, fathers were often merely fined for support of their "bastards," whereas women were "carted" and whipped, sometimes naked or in a shift, in the center of the village, a spectacle for all to see. Punishment was a scene, a spectacle that recognized the troubling power of a voracious female sexuality expressed through the fetishization of the female body. And that imagined voracious and punished body is both the object of pity and of admiration, a spectacle at once of submission and troubling power.

In the later puritan texts, instead of repressive state and community power working itself out on the rebellious bodies of women, women were interpellated as subjects through an ideology of the family that represented "an imaginary relation of [women] to their real conditions of existence."[29] Women's subjectivity was regulated and constructed in line with ideologies of femininity most useful to the apparatuses of state power. Whereas in the early works women are controlled from the outside and their sexuality is openly recognized, even respected because powerful, in the later handbooks, sermons, and the like, the representations of women as dutiful and companionate and the suppression of their sexuality fashion a different feminine subjectivity. In Edmund Tilney's words, a husband should "steal away her private will, and appetite, so that of two bodies there may be only one heart." Cleaver is less romantic: "The husband ought not to be satisfied with the use of his wives body, but in that hee hath also the possession of her will and affections." John Wing articulates this change most forcefully: "We will let the *wicked Woman* passe for the present, seing the words of our Text, treate of no other but of her that is excellent."[30]

However differently the early and late discourses about women and the family manage femininity, both depend on the powers of representation, whether it be the spectacle of the punished female body or the demure depiction of a right marital relation. The importance of representation for the management of femininity is evident not only in these texts written for a middle class or elite audience but also in the textual remains that communicate the regulation of gender in early English village communities.[31] The representational character of punishment for women who transgress the laws of gender has its counterpart in the accounts of skimmingtons and charivaris from the period. The word "skimmington" seems to be derived from the kitchen utensil, a "skimming," with the suffix added, as in *simpleton,* to simulate a personal name. A skimmington was either a shrewish or adulterous wife, or alternatively, the husband of one. The term conflates the offending and offended parties and finally comes to represent the country ceremony or procession intended to ridicule such behavior. If a wife abused her husband by being domineering or by committing, or even being suspected of, adultery, the inhabitants of the village would masquerade as the wife or husband or carry effigies representing the offending parties. Accompanied by an improvised band making "rough music" with pots and pans and other domestic utensils, they would assemble outside the house of the offender, occasionally break in and beat the wife or duck her in the village pond using the ducking stool or "cucking" stool kept for that purpose.[32]

In the Middle Ages such rituals were linked to the transgression of various community norms—rigged weights and measures, watering down beer and the like—but in the mid-sixteenth century in England, such ceremonies become gender specific. And interestingly, in the late seventeenth century, and more and more frequently after 1700, they are directed against men, particularly wife-beaters.[33] In a description of one such skimmington, which took place in Wiltshire in 1618, a small group of young men from Callne came playing a drum to Iwemerford, where they were met at the village bridge by a certain Thomas Wells and his landlord, who asked them what they wanted. When they answered they had come for "a Skimmington dwelling there," Wells's landlord told them the report was false and asked them to depart, which they did; but about noon they

> came again...another drumer named Wm. Watt, & wth him
> three or fower hundred men, some like soldiers, armed with
> pieces and other weapons, & a man riding upon a horse, have-
> ing a white night cap upon his head, two shininge hornes hang-
> ing by his eares, & counterfayte beard upon his chine made of a
> deares tayle, a smocke upon the top of his garments & he rode
> upon a red horse wth a paire of potts under him...he & all his
> companye made a stand when they came just against thise ex-
> aminates howse, & then ye gunners shott of their pieces, pipes &
> hornes were sounded, together with cowbells & other smaller
> belles wch the company had amongst them, & rames hornes &
> buckes hornes carried upon forkes were then and there lifted
> up and showen...Thomas Wells, ye husband, locked ye streete
> doore & locked his Wife into his chamber where she lay, and ye
> company pressinge hard against his howse he opened ye street
> doore to see whether he could psuade ye Companye to departe
> from his howse, & psently ye parties above mencioned & divers
> others rushed in upon him...and brake open his chamber
> doore upon his wife & she offeringe to escape from them by
> climinge a paire of staires to goe up into an upper roome, Wm.
> Wellwin plucked her downe by ye heels...and then he and the
> rest tooke her up by ye armes & legges, and had her out
> through the hall into ye entrye, where being a wett hole, they

threw her downe into it & trod upon hir & beried her filthily
with durt, & did beate hir blacke & blewe in many places with an
intent...to have had hir, viz Agnes, out of their howse to ye horse-
men & to have sett hir up behind him to carry hir to Callne &
there washe hir in the cucking stoole, & if she would not be still
& sitt quietly, then to stuffe hir mouth wth greines.[34]

This tale of troubled gender relations, signed by Sir John
Hungerford, a justice of the peace for Wilts, reveals a great deal about
family politics and anxieties about gender and power in early modern
England. Politics and sexuality are indissolubly mixed; the
community's ritual action against the wife seeks not only to punish
but also to reestablish conventional modes of gender behavior.

We owe our account of this skimmington, as is so often the case,
to the fact that it went awry: the law was broken, a house forcibly
entered, and the wife assaulted, which led Wells to bring a complaint
against his neighbors. Because this account represents the plaintiff's
point of view, we also find exaggeration—the claim that there were
three or four hundred men. Iwemerford was a village of some ten or
twelve houses; Callne was a large town, but not large enough to send
as large a contingent as Wells describes. His testimony seeks to represent the skimmington as an act against civil order in order to make his
case. But of greater interest is the relationship between the community
and the family, what we term the public and the private, figured here.
The townsmen of Callne and villagers of Iwemerford assume their
right to interfere in Wells's family life; but their interference is not
entirely public because it is not sanctioned by authorities: Wells's landlord turns away the company and testifies on the plaintiff's behalf.

Similarly, the ducking stools occupied a liminal place: they were
maintained by village and town authorities but were often used by
crowds in similar ritual actions to punish transgressors of social
customs and codes rather than actual law breakers. Unlike other forms
of criminality, the punishment of women for the transgression of gender codes straddles the public and domestic spheres. Skimmingtons
were enacted not only against suspected adulteresses but against
scolds and shrews as well; and shrews, scolds, and so-called husband-
abusers were also regularly suspected of sexual misbehavior. The beat-

ing of Wells's wife, Agnes, the ducking of women for transgressing the sex-gender system, publicly punishes the female body, making it a spectacle and an exemplum from which all are exhorted to learn.

These discourses on marriage and related community sanctions must not be understood as simply "dominant," as constructing a passive, victimized female subject who is dominated by hegemonic powers from above, but in terms of what Foucault has called the "rule of the tactical polyvalence of discourses": "We must make allowance for the complex and unstable process whereby discourse can be both an instrument and an effect of power, but also a hindrance, a stumbling-block, a point of resistance and a starting point for an opposing strategy."[35] The early seventeenth century is not only the moment when the discourses that manage femininity proliferate; it is also the moment when women first begin to write and be published in England and when women begin to play a larger role in the sectarian politics which led to the English civil war.[36] Though there is no question that Renaissance discourses of femininity advanced social controls and the policing of female behavior, they also enabled opposing discourses, which though they often speak with the same vocabulary and from the same categories, were nevertheless tactically productive.

In December 1648 and January 1649, a certain Elizabeth Poole, widow, testified before the Council of the Army concerning a dream purportedly about *not* executing Charles I; her account illustrates how familial analogies could be appropriated by the non-elite in unexpected ways:

> The King is your Father and husband, which you were and are to obey in the Lord, and no other way, for when he forgot his subordination to divine Fatherhood and headship, thinking he had begotten you a generation to his own pleasure, and taking you a wife for his own lusts, thereby is the yoke taken from your necks....You have all that you have and are, and although he would not be your father and husband, Subordinate, but Absolute, yet know that you are for the Lord's sake to honour his person....And although this bond is broken on his part; You never heard that a wife might put away her husband, as he is the head of her body....And accordingly you may hold the hands of your

husband, that he pierce not your bowels with a knife or sword to take your life. Neither may you take his...[37]

Poole figures the relationship of parliament to king as a failing marriage with parliament feminized as the wife. Here the binary oppositions of the manuals, husband/wife, love/obedience, active/passive, are refigured through a causal logic of non sequiturs: the "wife" is to obey her husband, but the yoke is taken from her neck; he would not be your "husband," yet you are to honor him.[38] Poole represents the king/husband with a paradox, subordinate/absolute, and emphasizes his "subordination to divine Fatherhood." In Poole's speech, the marital analogy is a hindrance to patriarchal conceptions of the state, "a point of resistance and a starting point for an opposing strategy." It is no accident that the 1640s were also the moment of the divorce debates and of the sectarian attacks on traditional ideologies of the family, sex, and marriage.[39] The radical movements and sectarianism of the 1640s and 1650s provide women increasingly with positions outside the family from which to speak. Though they continue to use discourses of marriage and the family to conceptualize political relationships and the state, that familial rhetoric is different; the relations it describes are far from the hypostasized models of the household manuals that proffered the illusion of an unchanging natural form.

Family politics, in ideological texts like the marriage sermons and conduct books I have analyzed and in the social rituals of the Elizabethan and Jacobean village, played a prominent role in early modern England. But troubled gender relations were not always managed within the idealized boundaries of the how-to book or by the rough "justice" of the crowd. On stage, women are frequently represented transgressing conventional social roles, but not necessarily punished for doing so. Drama stands in a liminal position, neither fully a part of the printed textual world of the elite nor wholly popular; and its generic conventions and rhetorical tropes problematize its representations of femininity.

THREE

# Renaissance Family Politics and Shakespeare's Taming of the Shrew

*A quarrel may end wi' the whip, but it begins wi' the tongue, and it's the women have got the most o' that.*
George Eliot, *Daniel Deronda*

W etherden, Suffolk. Plough Monday, 1604. A drunken tanner, Nicholas Rosyer, staggers home from the alehouse. On arriving at his door, he is greeted by his wife with "dronken dogg, pisspott and other unseemly names." When Rosyer tried to come to bed to her, she "still raged against him and badd him out dronken dog dronken pisspott." She struck him several times, clawed his face and arms, spit at him, and beat him out of bed. Rosyer retreated, returned to the alehouse, and drank until he could hardly stand up. Shortly thereafter, Thomas Quarry and others met and "agreed amongest themselfs that the said Thomas Quarry who dwelt at the next howse...should...ryde abowt the towne upon a cowlstaff whereby not onley the woman which had offended might be shunned for her misdemeanors towards her husband but other women also by her shame might be admonished to offence in like sort."[1] Domestic violence, far from being contained in the family, spills out into the neighborhood, and the response of the community is an "old country ceremony used in merriment upon such accidents."

Quarry, wearing a kirtle or gown and apron, "was carryed to diverse places and as he rode did admonishe all wiefs to take heede how they did beate their husbands." The Rosyers' neighbors reenacted their troubled gender relations: the beating was repeated, with Quarry in woman's clothes playing Rosyer's wife, the neighbors standing in for the "abused" husband, and a rough music procession to the house of the transgressors. The result of this "merriment" suggests its darker purpose and the anxiety about gender relations its displays: the offending couple left the village in shame. The skimmington served its purpose by its ritual scapegoating of the tanner and more particularly his wife. Rosyer vented his anger by bringing charges against his neighbors in which he complained not only of scandal and disgrace to himself, "his wief and kyndred," but also of seditious "tumult and discention in the said towne."[2]

The entire incident figures the social anxiety about gender and power that characterizes Elizabethan culture. Like Simon Forman's dream of wish-fulfillment with Queen Elizabeth, this incident, in Louis Montrose's words, "epitomizes the indissolubly political and sexual character of the cultural forms in which [such] tensions might be represented and addressed."[3] The community's ritual action against

*Well worth to scurge, so weake A patch, And cause the Boyes there at make games.*
*Who w<sup>th</sup> so strong, A whore would match by ryding thus, to both their shames:*

FIGURE FIVE  "A skimmington," *English Customs*, plate 9.
By permission of the Folger Shakespeare Library.

the couple who transgress prevailing codes of gender behavior seeks
to reestablish those conventional modes of behavior—it seeks to sanc-
tion a patriarchal order. But at the same time, this "old country ceremony" subverts, by its re-presentation, its masquerade of the very
events its criticizes, by forcing the offending couple to recognize their
transgression through its dramatic enactment. The skimmington seeks
"in merriment" to reassert traditional gender behaviors that are naturalized in Elizabethan culture as divinely ordained; but it also
deconstructs that "naturalization" by its foregrounding of what is a
humanly constructed cultural product: the displacement of gender
roles in a dramatic representation.[4]

## FAMILY POLITICS

The events of Plough Monday 1604 have an uncanny relation to
Shakespeare's *Taming of the Shrew*, which might well be read as a theat-

FIGURE SIX  Thomas Cecil, *"A New Yeeres guift for shrews,"* broadside
(ca. 1620). By permission of the Trustees of the British Museum.

rical realization of such a community fantasy, the shaming and subjection of a shrewish wife. The so-called induction opens with the hostess
railing at the drunken tinker Sly, and their interchange figures him as
the inebriated tanner from Wetherden.[5] Sly is presented with two
"dreams," the dream he is a lord—a fantasy enacting traditional Elizabethan hierarchical and gender relations—and the "dream" of
Petruchio taming Kate. The first fantasy is a series of artificially constructed power relationships figured first in terms of class, then in
terms of gender. The lord exhorts his servingmen to offer Sly "low
submissive reverence" and traditional lordly prerogatives and pursuits:
music, painting, handwashing, rich apparel, hunting, and finally a

RENAISSANCE  FAMILY  POLITICS

37

theatrical entertainment. In the longer, more detailed speech that follows in the induction at i, 100ff., he exhorts his page to "bear himself with honourable action/Such as he hath observ'd in noble ladies/Unto their lords." Significantly, Sly is only convinced of his lordly identity when he is told of his "wife." His realization of this newly discovered self involves calling for the lady, demanding from her submission to his authority, and finally seeking to exert his new power through his husbandly sexual prerogative: "Madam, undress you and come now to bed" (induct., ii, 118). By enacting Sly's identity as a lord through his wife's social and sexual (if deferred) submission, the induction suggests ironically how in this androcentric culture men depended on women to authorize their sexual and social masculine identities.[6] The lord's fantasy takes the drunken Sly who brawls with the hostess and by means of a "play" brings him into line with traditional conceptions of gender relations. But in the induction, these relationships of power and gender, which in Elizabethan treatises, sermons, homilies, and behavioral handbooks were figured as natural and divinely ordained, are subverted by the metatheatrical foregrounding of such roles and relations as culturally constructed.

The analogy between the events at Wetherden and Shakespeare's play suggests a tempting homology between history and cultural artifacts. It figures patriarchy as a master narrative, the key to understanding certain historical events and dramatic plots. But as Fredric Jameson points out, "history is not a narrative, master or otherwise, but . . . an absent cause. . .inaccessible to us except in textual form, and . . . our approach to it and to the Real itself necessarily passes through its prior textualization, its narrativization in the political unconscious."[7] If we return to Nicholas Rosyer's complaint against his neighbors and consider its textualization—how it is made accessible to us through narrative—we can make several observations. We notice immediately that Rosyer's wife, the subject of the complaint, lacks the status of a speaking subject. She is unnamed and referred to only as the "wief." Rosyer's testimony, in fact, begins with a defense not of his wife but of his patrimony, an account of his background and history in the village in terms of male lineage. His wife has no voice; typically, she never speaks in the complaint at all. Her husband brings charges against his neighbors presumably to clear his name and to affirm his identity as patriarch, which the incident itself, from his wife's "abuse" to the transvestite skimmington, endangers.

From the account of this case, we also get a powerful sense of life in early modern England, the close proximity of neighbors and the way intimate sexual relations present a scene before an audience. Quarry and the neighbors recount Rosyer's attempted assertion of his sexual "prerogatives" over his wife and her vehement refusal: "she struck him several times, clawed his face and arms, spit at him and beat him out of bed." There is evidently no place in the late Elizabethan sex/gender system for Rosyer's wife to complain of her husband's mistreatment, drunkenness, and abuse, or even to give voice to her point of view, her side of the story. The binary opposition between male and female in the Wetherden case and its figuration of patriarchy in early modern England generates the possible contradictions logically available to both terms: Rosyer speaks, his wife is silent; Rosyer is recognized as a subject before the law, his wife is solely its object; Rosyer's family must be defended against the insults of his neighbors, his wife has no family but has become part of his. In turning to *The Taming of the Shrew*, our task is to articulate the particular sexual/political fantasy, or, in Jameson's Althusserian formulation, the "libidinal apparatus" the play projects as an imaginary resolution of contradictions that are never resolved in the Wetherden case, but which the formal structures of dramatic plot and character in Shakespeare's play present as seemingly reconciled.

## A SHREW'S HISTORY

Many readers of Shakespeare's *Shrew* have noted that both in the induction and the play, language is an index of identity. Sly is convinced of his lordly identity by language, by the lord's obsequious words and recital of his false history. Significantly, when he believes himself a lord, his language changes and he begins to speak the blank verse of his retainers. But in the opening scene of the play proper, Shakespeare emphasizes not just the relationship between language and identity but that between control over language and fatherly authority. Kate's linguistic protest is against the role in patriarchal culture to which women are assigned, that of wife and object of exchange in the circulation of male desire. Her very first words make this point aggressively: she asks of her father, "I pray you, sir, is it your will/To make a stale of me amongst these mates?"[8] Punning on the meaning of stale as laughing stock and prostitute, on "stalemate," and on mate as husband, Kate refuses her erotic destiny by exercising a linguistic willfulness. Her shrewishness testifies to her exclusion from social and political power. Bianca, by contrast, is throughout the play associated with silence (I, i, 70–71).[9]

Kate's prayer to her father is motivated by Gremio's threat "to cart her rather. She's too rough for me" (I, i, 55). Although this line is usually glossed as "drive around in an open cart (a punishment for prostitutes)," the case of Nicholas Rosyer and his unnamed wife provides a more complex commentary. During the period from 1560 until the English Civil War, in which many historians have recognized a "crisis of order" in early modern England, the fear that women were rebelling against their traditional subservient role in patriarchal culture was widespread.[10] Popular works such as *The Two Angry Women of Abington* (1598), Middleton's *The Roaring Girl* (1611), *Hic Mulier,* or *The Man-Woman* (1620), and Joseph Swetnam's *Arraignment of lewd idle froward and inconstant women* (which went through ten editions between 1616 and 1634), all testify to a preoccupation with rebellious women.[11] What literary historians have recognized in late Elizabethan and Jacobean writers as a preoccupation with female rebellion and independence, social historians have also noted in historical records. As David Underdown has observed, the period was fraught with anxiety about rebellious women and particularly their rebellion through language.[12] Although men were occasionally charged with scolding, it was predominately a female offense usually associated with class as well as gender issues and revolt: "women who were poor, social outcasts, widows, or otherwise, lacking in the protection of a family...were the most common offenders."[13] Underdown points out that in a few examples after the Restoration, social disapproval shifts to "mismatched couples, sexual offenders, and eventually...husbands who beat their wives."[14] Punishment for such offenses and related ones involving "domineering" wives who "beat" or "abused" their husbands often involved public shaming or charivari of the sort employed at Wetherden and Callne. The accused woman or her surrogate was put in a scold's collar or ridden in a cart accompanied by a rough musical procession of villagers banging pots and pans.

Louis Montrose attributes the incidence of troubled gender relations to female rule since "all forms of public and domestic authority in Elizabethan England were vested in men: in fathers, husbands, masters, teachers, magistrates, lords. It was inevitable that the rule of a woman would generate peculiar tensions within such a patriarchal society."[15] Historians point to the social and economic factors that contributed to these troubled gender relations. Underdown observes a breakdown of community in fast-growing urban centers and scattered pasture/dairy parishes where effective means of social control such as compact nucleated village centers, resident squires, and strong manorial institutions were weak or nonexistent. He observes the higher incidence of troubled gender relations in such communities as opposed to the arable parishes, which "tended to retain strong habits of neighborhood and cooperation." Both Montrose's reading of the Elizabethan sex/gender system in terms of the "pervasive cultural presence" of the queen and Underdown's analysis of economic and social factors help to explain this proliferation of accusations of witchcraft, shrewishness, and husband domination. Both demonstrate the clear connection between women's independent appropriation of speech and a conceived threat to patriarchal authority contained through public shaming or spectacle—the ducking stool, usually called the cucking stool, or carting.[16]

From the outset of Shakespeare's play, Katherine's threat to male authority is posed through language; it is perceived as such by others and is linked to a claim larger than shrewishness—witchcraft—through the constant allusions to Katherine's kinship with the devil.[17] Control of women and particularly of Kate's revolt is from the outset attempted by inscribing women in a scopic economy.[18] Woman is represented as spectacle (Kate) or object to be desired and admired, a vision of beauty (Bianca). She is the site of visual pleasure, whether on the public stage, the village green, or the fantasy "cart" with which Hortensio threatens Kate. The threat of being made a spectacle, here by carting or later in the wedding scene by Petruchio's "mad-brain rudesby," is an important aspect of shrew-taming.[19] Given the evidence of social history and of the play itself, language is power, both in

Elizabethan and Jacobean England and in the fictional space of the *Shrew.*

The *Shrew* both demonstrated and helped produce the patriarchal social formation that characterized Elizabethan England, but representation gives us a perspective on that system that subverts its status as natural. The theatrically constructed frame in which Sly exercises patriarchal power and the dream in which Kate is tamed undermine the seemingly eternal nature of those structures by calling attention to the constructed character of the representation rather than veiling it through mimesis. The foregrounded female protagonist of the action and her powerful annexation of traditionally male discursive domains distances us from that system by exposing and displaying its contradictions. Representation undermines the ideology about women that the play presents and produces, both in the induction and in the Kate/Petruchio plot: Sly disappears as lord, but Kate keeps talking.

### THE PRICE OF SILENCE

At II, i, in the spat between Bianca and Kate, the relationship between silence and women's place in the marriage market is made clear. Kate questions Bianca about her suitors, inquiring as to her preferences. Some critics have read her questions and her abuse of Bianca (in less than thirty lines, Kate binds her sister's hands behind her back, strikes her, and chases after her calling for revenge) as revealing her secret desire for marriage and for the praise and recognition afforded her sister.[20] Kate's behavior may invite such an interpretation, but her questions and badgering also expose the relationship between Bianca's sweet sobriety and her success with men. Kate's abuse may begin as a jest, but her feelings are aroused to a different and more serious pitch when her father enters, taking as usual Bianca's part against her sister. Baptista emphasizes both Bianca's silence, "When did she cross thee with a bitter word?" and Katherine's link with the devil, "thou hilding of a devilish spirit" (II, i, 28, 26). We should bear in mind here Underdown's observation that shrewishness is a class as well as gender issue, that women "lacking in the protection of a family...were the most common offenders."[21] Kate is motherless, and virtually fatherless as well, for Baptista consistently rejects her and favors her obedient sister. Kate's threat that follows, "Her silence flouts me, and I'll be reveng'd" (II, i, 29) reveals that silence has insured Bianca's place in the male economy of desire and exchange to which Kate pointedly refers in her last lines:

What, will you not suffer me? Nay, now I see
She is your treasure, she must have a husband,
I must dance barefoot on her wedding day,
And, for your love to her lead apes in hell.
(II, i, 31–34)

Throughout the play, Bianca is a treasure, a jewel, an object of desire and possession. Although much has been made of the animal analogies between Kate and beasts, the metaphorical death of the courtly imagery associated with Bianca has been ignored as too conventional, if not natural, to warrant comment.[22] At issue here is not so much Kate's lack of a husband, or indeed her desire for a marriage partner, but rather her distaste at those folk customs that make her otherness, her place outside the sex/gender system, a public fact, a spectacle for all to see and mock.

In the battle of words between Kate and Petruchio at II, i, 182ff., it is Kate who gets the best of her suitor. She takes the lead through puns that allow her to criticize Petruchio and patriarchal practices of wooing and marriage. Her sexual puns make explicit to the audience not so much her secret preoccupation with sex and marriage but what is implicit in Petruchio's wooing: that marriage is a sexual exchange in which women are exploited for their use-value as producers. Significantly, Petruchio's language is linguistically similar to Kate's in its puns and wordplay. He also presents her, as many commentators have noted, with an imagined vision that makes her conform to the very order against which she rebels: he makes her a Bianca with words, shaping an identity for her that confirms the social expectations of the sex/gender system that informs the play.

In the altercation over staying for the wedding feast after their marriage, Kate again claims the importance of language and her use of it to women's place and independence in the world. But here it is

Petruchio who controls language, who has the final word, for he creates through words a situation to justify his actions: he claims to be rescuing Kate from thieves. More precisely, he claims she asks for the rescue. Kate's annexation of speech does not work unless her audience, and particularly her husband, accepts what she says as independent rebellion. By deliberately misunderstanding and reinterpreting her words to suit his own ends, Petruchio effectively refuses her the freedom of speech identified in the play with her independence. Such is his strategy throughout this central portion of the action, in their arrival at his house, and in the interchange with the tailor. Kate is figuratively killed with kindness, by her husband's rule over her not so much in material terms—the withholding of food, clothing and sleep—but in the withholding of linguistic understanding. As the receiver of her messages, he simply refuses their meaning; since he also has material power to enforce his interpretations, it is his power over language that wins.

In the exchange between Petruchio and Kate with the tailor, Kate makes her strongest bid yet for linguistic freedom:

> Why, sir, I trust I may have leave to speak,
> And speak I will. I am no child, no babe.
> Your betters have endur'd me say my mind,
> And if you cannot, best you stop your ears.
> My tongue will tell the anger of my heart,
> Or else my heart concealing it will break,
> And rather than it shall, I will be free
> Even to the uttermost, as I please, in words.
> (IV, iii, 73–80)

When we next encounter Kate, however, on the journey to Padua, she finally admits to Petruchio: "What you will have it nam'd, even that it is,/And so it shall be so for Katherine" (IV, v, 21–22). On this journey Kate calls the sun the moon, an old man a budding virgin, and makes the world conform to the topsy-turvy of Petruchio's patriarchal whimsy. But we should look carefully at this scene before acquiescing in too easy a view of Kate's submission. Certainly she gives in to Petruchio's demands literally; but her playfulness and irony here are indisputable. As she says at IV, v, 44–48:

Pardon, old father, my mistaking eyes,
That have been so bedazzled with the sun
That everything I look on seemeth green.
Now I perceive thou art a reverend father.
Pardon, I pray thee, for my mad mistaking.

Given Kate's talent for puns, we must understand her line, "bedazzled with the sun," as a pun on son and as play with Petruchio's line earlier in the scene "Now by my mother's son, and that's myself,/It shall be moon, or star, or what I list" (IV, v, 6–7). "Petruchio's bedazzlement" is exactly that, and Kate here makes clear the playfulness of their linguistic games.

In his paper "Hysterical Phantasies and Their Relation to Bi-Sexuality" (1908), Freud observes that neurotic symptoms, particularly the hysterical symptom, have their origins in the daydreams of adolescence.[23] "In girls and women," Freud claims, "they are invariably of an erotic nature, in men they may be either erotic or ambitious."[24] A feminist characterological rereading of Freud might suggest that Kate's ambitious fantasies, which her culture allows her to express only in erotic directions, motivate her shrewishness.[25] Such behavior, which in a man would not be problematic, her family and peers interpret as "hysterical," diabolic, or both. Her "masculine" behavior saves her, at least for a time, from her feminine erotic destiny.

Freud goes on to claim that hysterical symptoms are always bisexual, "the expression of both a masculine and a feminine unconscious sexual phantasy."[26] The example he gives is a patient who "pressed her dress to her body with one hand (as the woman) while trying to tear it off with the other (as the man)."[27] To continue our "analysis" in the scene we are considering, we might claim that Kate's female masquerade obscures her continuing ambitious fantasies, now only manifest in the puns and ironic wordplay that suggest the distance between her character and the role she plays.[28] Even though she gives up her shrewishness and acquiesces to Petruchio's whims, she persists in her characteristic "masculine" linguistic exuberance while masquerading as an obedient wife.[29]

Instead of using Freud to analyze Kate's character, a critical move of debatable interpretive power, we might consider the Freudian text instead as a reading of ideological or cultural patterns. The process Freud describes is suggestive for analyzing the workings not of character but of Shakespeare's text itself. No speech in the play has been more variously interpreted than Kate's final speech of women's submission. In a useful essay on the *Shrew,* John Bean has conveniently assigned to the two prevailing views the terms "revisionist" for those who would take Kate's speech as ironic and her subservience as pretense—a way of living peacefully in patriarchal culture but with an unregenerate spirit—and "anti-revisionist" for those who argue that farce is the play's governing genre and that Kate's response to Petruchio's taming is that of an animal responding to "the devices of a skilled trainer."[30] Bean himself argues convincingly for a compromise position that admits the "background of depersonalizing farce unassimilated from the play's fabliau sources" but suggests that Kate's taming needs to be seen in terms of romantic comedy, as a spontaneous change of heart such as those of the later romantic comedies "where characters lose themselves in chaos and emerge, as if from a dream, liberated into the bonds of love."[31] Bean rightly points out the liberal aspects of the final speech in which marriage is seen as a partnership as well as a hierarchy, citing the humanist writers on marriage and juxtaposing Kate's speech with corresponding, and remarkably more misogynist, lines in *The Taming of a Shrew* and other taming tales.[32]

Keeping in mind Bean's arguments for the content of the speech and its place at the intersection of farce and romantic love plot, I would like to turn to its significance as representation. What we find is Katherine as a strong, energetic female protagonist represented before us addressing not the onstage male audience, only too aware of its articulation of patriarchal power, but Bianca and the Widow, associated with silence throughout the play and finally arriving by means, as Petruchio calls it, of Kate's "womanly persuasion" (V, ii, 120).

Unlike any other of Shakespeare's comedies, we have here represented not simply marriage, with the final curtain a veiled mystification of the sexual and social results of that ritual, but a view, however brief and condensed, of that marriage over time.[33] And what we see is not a quiet and submissive wife but the same energetic and linguistically active Kate with which the play began. We know, then, in a way we never know about the other comedies—except perhaps *The Merchant of Venice,* and there our knowledge is complicated by Portia's male disguise—that Kate has continued to speak. She has not, of course, continued to speak her earlier language of revolt and anger. Instead she has adopted another strategy, a strategy the French psychoanalyst Luce Irigaray calls mimeticism.[34] Irigaray argues that women are cut off from language by the patriarchal order in which they live, by their entry into the Symbolic, which the Father represents in a Freudian-Lacanian model.[35] Women's only possible relation to the dominant discourse is mimetic:

> To play with mimesis is...for a woman to try to recover the place of her exploitation by language, without allowing herself to be simply reduced to it. It is to resubmit herself...to ideas—notably about her—elaborated in and through a masculine logic, but to "bring out" by an effect of playful repetition what was to remain hidden: the recovery of a possible operation of the feminine in language. It is also to unveil the fact that if women mime so well they are not simply reabsorbed in this function. They also remain elsewhere.[36]

Whereas Irigaray goes on to locate this "elsewhere" in sexual pleasure (*jouissance*), Nancy Miller has elaborated on this notion of "mimeticism," describing it as a "form of emphasis: an italicized version of what passes for the neutral....Spoken or written, italics are a modality of intensity and stress; a way of marking what has already been said, of making a common text one's own."[37] Interestingly it is Bianca, revealed once married as herself a "shrew," who perhaps most memorably appropriates dominant discourse and italicizes it in the conventional wooing scene at III, i. There Lucentio construes lines from Ovid's *Heroides* to reveal his identity and love; Bianca playfully repeats them to discover her own anxieties and feelings.

Joel Fineman has observed the difficulty in distinguishing between man's and woman's speech in the *Shrew* by demonstrating how the rhetorical strategies Kate deploys are like Petruchio's.[38] But Kate's self-consciousness about the power of language, her punning and irony, and her techniques of linguistic masquerade, are strategies of italics—mimetics strategies, in Irigaray's sense of mimeticism. Instead of figuring an essentialized woman's speech, they deform language by subverting it, that is, by turning it inside out so that metaphors, puns, and other forms of wordplay manifest their veiled equivalences: the meaning of woman as treasure, of wooing as a civilized and acceptable disguise for sexual exploitation, of the objectification and exchange of women. Kate's speech contradicts the very sentiments she affirms; rather than resolve the play's action, her monologue simply displays the fundamental contradiction presented by a female dramatic protagonist, between woman as a sexually desirable silent object and women of words, women with power over language who disrupt, or at least italicize, women's place and part in Elizabethan culture.

To dramatize action involving linguistically powerful women characters militates against Tudor and Stuart ideologies of women's silence. To maintain their status as desirable, Shakespeare's heroines frequently must don male attire in order to speak: Rosalind, Portia, even the passive Viola. The conflict between the explicitly repressive content of Kate's speech and the implicit message of independence communicated by representing a powerful female protagonist speaking the play's longest speech at a moment of emphatic suspense is not unlike Freud's female patient who "pressed her dress to her body with one hand (as the woman) while trying to tear it off with the other (as the man)." We might even say that this conflict shares the bisexuality Freud claims for the hysterical symptom, that the text itself is sexually ambivalent, a view in keeping with the opposed readings of the play in which it is either conservative farce or subversive irony. Such a representation of gender, what might be termed the "female dramatizable,"[39] is always at once patriarchally suspect and sexually ambivalent, clinging to Elizabethan patriarchal ideology and at the same time tearing it away by foregrounding or italicizing its constructed character.

### Missing Frames and Female Spectacles

Kate's final speech exemplifies what Jameson describes as "imaginary or formal 'solutions' to unresolvable social contradictions," but the appearance of resolution is an "ideological mirage."[40] On the level of plot, as many readers have noted, if one shrew is tamed, two more reveal themselves. Bianca and the widow refuse to do their husbands' bidding, thereby undoing the sense of closure Kate's "acquiescence" produces. By articulating the contradiction manifested in the scene's formal organization and its social "content"—between the "headstrong women," now Bianca and the widow who refuse their duty, and Kate and her praise of women's submission—the seeming resolution of the play's ending is exploded and its heterogeneity rather than its unity is foregrounded. But can a staged transgression of the law of women's silence be subversive? It is, after all, a theoretical commonplace to argue that transgression presupposes norms or taboos. Anthropologists have claimed that such ritual transgression insures order and stability; and literary critics, influenced by anthropology and a fashionable cultural pessimism that skirts the reactionary, argue that such subversion is always already contained.[41] The "female dramatizable," then, would be no more than a means of managing troubled gender relations, the fabled safety valve. By transgressing the law of women's silence, far from subverting it, the *Shrew* reconfirms the law, if we remember that Kate, Bianca, and the widow remain the object of the audience's gaze, specular images, represented female bodies on display, as on the cucking stool or in the cart. Representation contains female rebellion. And because the play has no final framing scene, no return to Sly, it could be argued that its artifice is relaxed, that the final scene is experienced naturalistically. The missing frame allows the audience to forget that Petruchio's taming of Kate is presented as a fiction.

Yet even with its missing frame and management of woman through spectacle, the *Shrew* deconstructs its own mimetic effect if we remember the bisexual aspect of the representation of women on the Elizabethan and Jacobean stage. In the early modern period, when women's behavior was closely circumscribed, containing operations such as generic closure—the tamings in shrew tales, the weddings that end other of Shakespeare's comedies, the convention of the boy actor—might be understood as enabling conditions for the foregrounding of transgression. Such operations, however, can never "retrospectively guarantee ideological erasure" of contestatory voices.[42] Kate would have been played by a boy whose transvestism, like Thomas Quarry's in the Wetherden skimmington, emblematically embodied the sexual contradictions manifest both in the play and Elizabethan culture. The very indeterminateness of the actor's sexuality, of the woman/man's body, the supplementarity of its titillating homo-erotic play (Sly's desire for the page boy disguised as a woman, Petruchio's "Come Kate, we'll to bed"), foregrounds its artifice and therefore subverts the play's patriarchal master narrative by exposing it as neither natural nor divinely ordained, but culturally constructed.

CHAPTER THREE

# FOUR

# Discovering Witches: Sorciographics

*For my part, I have ever believed*
*(and do now know) that there are witches.*[1]
  Sir Thomas Browne, *Religio medici*

*Your hands are not your own,*
*nor are your breasts, nor, most especially,*
*any of your bodily orifices, which we*
*may explore or penetrate at will....*
*you have lost all right to privacy or concealment...*
  The Story of O

*A* t Act I, v, of *Macbeth,* Lady Macbeth responds to news of the weird sisters' prophecies and Duncan's arrival with a famous, if not notorious, soliloquy, in which she imperates,

> Come to my woman's breasts,
> And take my milk for gall, you murth'ring ministers,
> Wherever in your sightless substances
> You wait on nature's mischief!

When read in the context of English witchcraft, this passage links "Macbeth's wife," as the Folio identifies her, directly with the witches. The short dialogue that opens the play, in which the weird sisters promise to meet Macbeth on the heath and then depart at the call of "Gray-Malkin" and "Paddock," immediately evokes the witch lore of early modern England. From the cases in the early years of Elizabeth's reign to the notorious Lancashire trials of 1612 and 1634–35 to the infamous doings in 1645 of Matthew Hopkins of Essex, witchfinder, the "discoverie" of witches consistently involved finding out their "familiars," the devil's agents who did their bidding: killing livestock, murdering neighbors, spoiling beer.

These spirits were believed to take on various shapes, most often of animals such as toads, birds, cats or dogs, and to require regular nourishment from their dams. Typically they had names like Sathan or Pluck or Crowe, homely appellations like Sack or Sugar, or Suckin' or Greedigut, and were often explicitly represented as children of the witch. "Familiars" were fed blood or milk from extra teats or "bigges" believed to mark the witch's body, often on her "privie parts"—supernumerary nipples were reportedly identified on the *pudenda* of almost all the Lancashire witches but might be located anywhere, including on feet, under arms, even in the hair. As early as 1579, such marks were said to be a "common token to know all witches by."[2] A suspected witch was searched for these telltale teats and for other marks of the devil. Since such marks were believed to be immune from pain, part of the discovery of a witch often involved the pricking of these spots with evil-looking, phallic instruments. In Scotland and occasionally in England, the finding of witches even produced a special occupation, "witchfinder" or "pricker." There were even retractable prickers that fraudulent witchfinders used to prove a witch's guilt by demonstrating that she did not feel pain in her marks.

As such operations suggest, witchcraft was a *crimen exceptum,* an exceptional crime not subject to the usual standards of proof, interrogation, and procedure, which required a confession or the testimony of direct witnesses. No one had to see a crime committed; instead witnesses could testify merely as to motives and effects. As a leading manual for justices of the peace of the period phrased it, "half proofes are to be allowed, and are good causes of suspition."[3] In a witchcraft trial, it was "lawful to give in Evidence Matters that are no ways relating to that Fact, and done many Years before"; even absence from the scene of the crime was irrelevant. The point I want to emphasize here is what the social historian Christina Larner notes as a "constant peculiarity of witch prosecuting. Suspects are never obvious; they have always to be found and identified,"[4] or in sixteenth-century terminology, "discovered."

Historians have elaborated the complex social factors that led over time to the denunciation, prosecution, and punishment of witches in early modern England. Causes have been endlessly debated and were clearly several. One account, which could be termed the scapegoat theory, argues that the persecution of deviance is characteristic of a new regime, religious or secular, seeking to establish itself.[5] Another explanation advanced by Keith Thomas and Alan Macfarlane is the widely accepted social strain theory or "functional" interpretation, attributing the increased number of witchcraft accusations and prosecutions to village tensions produced by social, economic, and demographic changes: the loss of Roman Catholic ritual and protective ecclesiastical magic, a breakdown in community relations, neighborliness and hospitality, the bureaucratization of poor relief, and a newly developing commercial ethic.[6]

Both Thomas and Macfarlane relate story after story in which an old woman begs at the door of her more fortunate neighbor, is rebuffed, and mutters a curse; some months later some catastrophe befalls the household of the neighbor, and he or she accuses the old woman of witchcraft. Both quote George Gifford's evocative description of this process in his *Discourse of the Subtill Practises of Devilles by Witches and Sorcerers* (1587):

> Some woman doth fal out bitterly with her neighbour: there followeth some great hurt....There is a suspicion conceived. Within fewe yeares after shee is in some iarre with an other. Hee is also plagued. This is noted of all. Great fame is spread of the matter. Mother W. is a witch. She hath bewitched goodman B. Two hogges which died strangely: or else hee is taken lame. Wel, mother W doth begin to bee very odious & terrible unto many. her neighbours, dare say nothing but yet in their heartes they wish shee were hanged.7

This operation, which sociologists call labeling, takes place over a period of years.[8] Neighbors build up resentments, they gossip, scapegoat, and in the end, old Mother W "is arrayned and condemned." Macfarlane observes that the character of the suspect was particularly important in witchcraft proceedings: the "likelihood of guilt was related to the whole social background of the accused: his parents' character, his friendships, drinking habits, and general reputation."

What is extraordinary about Macfarlane's observation here are the pronouns: *his, his*. Statistically in England witches were overwhelmingly women—over 90 percent. Not only the character of the suspect, as Macfarlane phrases it, but the sex of the suspect, was crucial. The few men tried for witchcraft in England were almost always related to known witches or rounded up in some of the larger multiple hunts that encompassed not only the accused but the accused's family.[9] Reginald Scot, in his useful compilation of witchcraft lore published in 1584, observes "at this day it is indifferent to say in the English tongue 'she is a witch' or 'she is a wise woman.'"[10] In Thomas's important study of English witchcraft, *Religion and the Decline of Magic*, he quotes Scot to emphasize that "there was no special term to indicate maleficient magicians," a point he uses to prove his own larger argument that witchcraft was part of an entire system of beliefs that included religion, magic, astrology, fairies, healing, and so forth. But in so doing, Thomas, like Macfarlane, ignores the shared salient feature of Scot's two phrases, "she is a witch" and "she is a wise woman": the feminine pronoun. Though the practitioners of English witchcraft were almost always women, historians have too often ignored the gender specificity of sixteenth- and seventeenth-century English witchcraft.[11]

Why? Christina Larner begins her discussion of this question with an anecdote. Organizers of an unemployment rally in Britain, she recounts, suggested "Ditch the Witch" as a campaign slogan. A Labour Party member, a schoolgirl it happens, objected. The alternative was "Ditch the Bitch," at which point, Larner tells us, the schoolgirl apparently gave up.

> The same week the death of an elderly woman from starvation was reported in the press. It was noted that she had been the bane of the social work department for years, refusing offers of help, asserting her privacy and independence, and abusing all those who came near her. The report also noted that the local children called her "the witch." Only the children? And what do the Prime Minister and a pauperized escapee from the welfare state have in common?
>   The stereotype witch is an independent adult woman who does not conform to the male idea of proper female behaviour. She is assertive; she does not require or give love...she does not nurture men or children, nor care for the weak. She has the power of words—to defend herself or to curse.[12]

Not only were the practitioners of witchcraft in England women, they were often disorderly or unruly women who transgressed cultural codes of femininity. In his *Discoverie of Witchcraft* (1584), written to refute the belief in witches but which ironically seems rather to have gathered in one book much of the scattered witch lore of the period, Scot observed that witches were said to be "women which be commonly old, lame, bleare-eied, pale, fowle, and full of wrinkles; poore, sullen, superstitious, and papists; or such as knowe no religion....They are doting, scolds, mad, divelish" (4). Significantly, all those behaviors transgressing traditional gender codes were conflated—a witch typically was said to be a scold, a shrew; to "live unquietly with her husband"; to be a "light woman" or a "common harlot"—witches were regularly accused of sexual misconduct. In Rowley, Dekker, and Ford's *The Witch of Edmonton,* for example, the witch Mother Sawyer recognizes that the accusation of witchcraft is only part of a larger animus against all women which is displaced onto the poor, aged, and helpless:

Mother Sawyer.                 A Witch? who is not?
    Hold not that universal Name in scorne then.
    What are your painted things in Princes Courts?
    Upon whose Eye-lids Lust sits blowing fires
    To burn Mens Souls in sensual hot desires:
    Upon whose naked Paps, a Leachers thought
    Acts Sin in fouler shapes then can be wrought. . . .
    Have you not City-witches who can turn
    Their husbands wares, whole standing shops of wares
    To sumptuous Tables, Gardens of stoln sin?
    In one year wasting, what scarce twenty win.
    Are not these Witches?
Justice.                 Yes, yes, but the Law
    Casts not an eye on these.
Mother Sawyer.                 Why then on me,
    Or any lean old Beldame? Reverence once
    Had wont to wait on age. Now an old woman
    Ill favour'd grown with yeers, if she be poor,
    Must she be call'd Bawd or Witch. Such so abus'd
    Are the course Witches: t'other are the fine,
    Spun for the Devil's own wearing.
                                        (IV, i, 101–24)[13]

The "crisis of order" historians have recognized in early modern England, and particularly the challenges to traditional ideals of womanhood posed by the proliferation of printed books and increased literacy, as well as by demographic changes bringing about out-of-town apprenticeships or "service" and later marriage for women, led to a displacement of anxiety onto the woman, aggravated no doubt by a virgin queen without an heir. Historically, the consequence was a rise in witchcraft persecutions, presentments for scolding, shrewishness, and bastardy; or to put it differently, the consequence was the criminalization of women, the labeling of old behaviors in new ways. In her indictment in 1662, Margaret Lister of Fife was described as "a witch, a charmer and a libber" (literally, a gelder).[14] In the nineteenth century, as Foucault and others have observed, the consequence of technological and social change was the medicalization of the other, the "diagnosis" and naming of pathologies: homosexuality, hysteria, neurasthenia. Witch in early modern England, hysteric in the nineteenth century, bitch today—nonconforming women threaten hegemonic sex/gender systems.

But context, as Derrida has reminded us with important consequences for historical readings, is boundless; it is "never absolutely determinable...never certain or saturated."[15] There is always more to describe, no limit to what a given context might include. Derrida dramatizes the voluminous possibilities of further specifying context by pointing out the displacements allowed by the unconscious as it is elaborated in psychoanalysis. Historians describe the peculiar, even bizarre, indicators of English witchcraft—the witch's polymastic body, her filial familiars—and dismiss them as "mere incidentals," but these details suggest another context in which to read English witchcraft. The finding of teats, the pricking of the devil's marks, the suckling of filial familiars, the passing down of witchcraft lore from mother to daughter, the accusations leveled at mothers by their children, all adumbrate a peculiar narrative of motherhood and the unconscious. In early modern England, witchcraft represented an inversion of maternal relations, of the maternal body, and finally, the powerful ambivalence of the mother's body in its double capacity as sexual object and nurturing mother.[16]

In contemporary literary criticism, psychoanalysis is the privileged discourse of the maternal. To invoke the maternal seems to entail psychoanalysis, in the strong sense of the verb *entails: if* we read the maternal, *then* we use psychoanalysis. Within Shakespeare studies, this if-then implicature has been particularly powerful. In a recent review article, Linda Boose in fact claims that the methodology "most feminist scholars" brought to the study of Shakespeare was "psychoanalytic, a perspective that American feminists revised by shifting focus away from Freud's phallocentric paradigm toward an inclusion of the maternal issues of gender formation enunciated by theorists like Melanie

Klein, D. W. Winnicott, Nancy Chodorow, and Dorothy Dinnerstein."[17] English witchcraft cases and plays seem virtually to dictate a psychoanalytic approach of the kind Boose describes: Freud's theory of the role and function of the mother's breast in infantile development, later elaborated by Melanie Klein, offers a remarkably compelling narrative through which to read the discourses of English witchcraft.

"Sucking at his mother's breast, or at substitutes for it," Freud claimed, is "the child's first and most vital activity."[18] The breast is the first source of pleasure and gratification the infant experiences. Not only the alleviation of hunger but also the pleasure from sucking the mother's breast is essential to the child's development and sexuality. According to Klein, the frustration of that pleasure, the denial of the breast, provokes feelings of hatred and aggression which are directed

> towards the same object as are the pleasurable [feelings],
> namely, the breasts of the mother....Freud called this the "plea-
> sure-pain principle." Thus the breast of the mother which gives
> gratification or denies it becomes, in the mind of the child, im-
> bued with the characteristics of good and evil. Now, what one
> might call the "good" breasts become the prototype of what is
> felt throughout life to be good and beneficent, while the "bad"
> breasts stand for everything evil and persecuting. The reason for
> this can be explained by the fact that, when the child turns his
> hatred against the denying or "bad" breast, he attributes to the
> breast itself all his own active hatred against it—a process which
> is termed *projection*.[19]

Klein goes on to postulate that sadism, the fusion of fantasies of hostile aggression with those of erotic pleasure, is focused first on the mother's breasts but "gradually extend[s] to her whole body" (36). The woman's body, and particularly her breasts, are always ambivalent, the stage of love and hate, desire and revulsion. These feelings of hostility in normal development are worked out through a process she calls *reparation,* by which the child overcomes fear and anger and becomes socially integrated.

If we read the discourses of witchcraft in early modern England through Klein's Freudian paradigm, we can identify the witch persecutions of the late sixteenth and early seventeenth centuries as a projection of those earliest feelings of hatred and aggression against the mother. On the witch's body is mapped out the hated mother's breast in the "bigges" or teats used to feed her familiars. The sadism generated by the double feelings or fantasies of satisfaction and deprivation experienced at the mother's breast is worked out in the process of "discovering" witches—and here is the reason behind my epigraph from *The Story of O:* the woman's body is stripped, shaved, bound, penetrated and searched in every orifice, watched for visitations by her familiars, deprived of sleep, sustenance, and finally of life. The clergyman John Gaule, for example, records such a search for telltale teats and other marks of the devil by searchers or officials who,

> having taken the suspected witch...placed [her naked] in the middle of a room upon a stool, or Table, crosse-legg'd, or in some other uneasie posture, to which if she submits not, she is then bound with cords; there is she watcht and kept without meat or sleep for the space of 24 hours....A little hole is likewise made in the door for the Impe to come in at.[20]

The inverted maternal is worked out not only on the witch's body and in the tales of her family of "familiars" but intergenerationally within households. Typically children reported learning witch lore from their mothers or older female relatives, or alternatively they testified against them in trials. The earliest Elizabethan case, published in a pamphlet dated 1566, records the confessions of Elizabeth Francis and "Mother Waterhouse," as she is referred to in the records.[21] Francis testified that she learned the art of witchcraft from her grandmother, the aptly named Mother Eve of Hatfield Peverell. Her familiar, a cat named Satan, demanded a drop of her blood, which he sucked from a red spot on her body each time he acted on her behalf. Francis claimed to have kept the cat for fifteen or sixteen years before passing it on to a neighbor, one Agnes Waterhouse. Mother Waterhouse's eighteen-year-old daughter Jone was also accused and testified "that her mother this laste wynter woulde have learned her this arte, but she lerned it not" (Haining, 27). Once, she recounted, a neighbor having denied her bread and cheese, she summoned the imp Satan—now transformed into a toad—to frighten the neighbor. Afterwards, Jone testified, Satan "demanded her body," and afraid, she yielded. Though Jone escaped prosecution, her mother was hanged. Similarly, Elizabeth Francis, perhaps because she testified against Mother Waterhouse, was acquitted, but was brought to trial and executed thirteen years later along with the daughter of another previously executed witch, whose young son in turn testified against his mother. In the annals of English witchcraft, such filial behavior was not anomalous: records show that children, both juvenile and adult, frequently testified against their mothers or older female relatives in witchcraft trials.[22]

Through the grid of psychoanalysis, then, the witch hunts of early modern England can be read as a projection of hatred and aggression toward the mother, which is worked out through the persecution if not of the mother herself, of old, poor, or otherwise powerless women. The seductiveness of this interpretation is apparent in many of the witch plays of the period. The most common claim made about *Macbeth* is that a reversal or inversion of Duncan's "natural and orderly" rule is the key idea: Macbeth murders the king and disrupts that harmony, Lady Macbeth equates regicide with manliness and repudiates her womanhood.[23] No image of inverted motherhood is more powerful than her speech at I, vii:

> I have given suck, and know
> How tender 'tis to love the babe that milks me;
> I would, while it was smiling in my face,
> Have pluck'd my nipple from his boneless gums,
> And dash'd the brains out, had I so sworn as you
> Have done to this. (54–59)

Harry Berger claims these lines witness not merely Lady Macbeth's perversion, but the pervasive threat of the "terrible power of the mother. To be deprived of the milkly bond, to be left helpless," writes Berger, "brings on the milkiness of cream-faced, whey-faced fear" (27–28).

Janet Adelman elaborates these "Fantasies of Maternal Power in *Macbeth*" specifically in relation to witchcraft:

The play strikingly constructs the fantasy of subjection to maternal malevolence in two parts, in the witches and in Lady Macbeth, and then persistently identifies the two parts as one. Through this identification, Shakespeare in effect locates the source of his culture's fear of witchcraft in individual human history, in the infant's long dependence on female figures felt as all powerful: what the witches suggest about the vulnerability of men to female power on the cosmic plane, Lady Macbeth doubles on the psychological plane. (97)

The danger with Berger's and Adelman's readings, and with this psychoanalytic paradigm, is that it naturalizes hostility toward women—it is said to be a part of every child's development, a product of "the infant's long dependence on female figures felt as all powerful." Such a reading of witchcraft and *Macbeth* is troubling; it is situated in an essentialist epistemology, grounded in the woman's sexed body, that is complicitous with the very discourses it criticizes.[24] But Adelman's reading of *Macbeth* and witchcraft is most striking in its foregrounding of psychoanalysis's seemingly relentless and absolute excision of the social and historical: witchcraft is the product of "individual human history"; the play works on the "cosmic" and "psychological" planes.

Readings such as Berger's and Adelman's (they are representative, though particularly fine exemplars) assume that the term "mother" is ahistorical, that it has no history, just as sexuality, until recently, has been assumed to have no history but to be grounded in instincts, drives, needs, and desires that are shared across all kinds of spatial, temporal, and social divides.[25] But psychoanalysis need not inevitably make ahistorical claims about human development that preclude historical analysis.[26]

In *Life and Death in Psychoanalysis*, Jean Laplanche argues that sexuality has been mistakenly understood to emerge from "an elaborate theory of a relation with the mother" based on a misunderstanding of the Freudian concept *Anlehnung* (literally "to find support").[27] Translated as "anaclitic" first in "On Narcissism" but used by Freud frequently in his work on the instincts, "the term *propping*," Laplanche points out, "has been understood...as a leaning on the *object,* and ultimately a leaning on the mother," whereas in fact "it by no means designates a leaning of the subject on the object (of child on mother).... [but] a leaning *of the drive,* the fact that emergent sexuality attaches itself to and is propped upon another process," a vital function or need—nourishment—and not upon any specific object (16). Laplanche quotes from *Three Essays on the Theory of Sexuality* at length:

> At a time at which the first beginnings of sexual satisfaction are still linked with the taking of nourishment [i. e., in the propping phase], the sexual instinct has a sexual object outside the infant's own body in the shape of his mother's breast. It is only later that he loses it, just at the time, perhaps, when he is able to form a total idea of the person to whom the organ that is giving him satisfaction belongs. As a rule the sexual drive then becomes auto-erotic...and not until the period of latency has been passed through is the original relation restored. There are good reasons why a child sucking at his mother's breast has become the prototype of every relation of love. The finding of an object is in fact the re-finding of it. (19)

As Laplanche observes, "the object to be rediscovered is not the lost object, but its substitute by displacement...and the object one seeks to refind in sexuality is an object displaced in relation to that first object, since the object which has been lost *is not the same* as that which is to be rediscovered" (20).

Laplanche denaturalizes the family romance by emphasizing that the object in sexuality is unfixed, "the precarious result of a historical evolution which at every stage of its development may bifurcate differently" (15). Though he is speaking of individual development, Laplanche's observation need not be restricted to the sexual etiology of the individual. In the case at hand, it allows us to ask how the object of sexuality is socially and ideologically produced in a given culture. Laplanche's explication of Freud allows us both a theory of desire and the space to explore the historical and social formations that often made women, and particularly the mother or her substitute, the object of hatred and aggression in late sixteenth- and seventeenth-century England.

In her interesting essay "Writing and Motherhood," Susan Suleiman analyzes the psychoanalytic literature about motherhood that assumes, in Helene Deutsch's famous formulation, "mothers don't write, they are written." In the psychoanalytic formula, mothers have babies, not books; they write only when they cannot have a child instead, or alternatively, when their reproductive history is behind them, what Suleiman wittily calls the "menopausal theory of artistic creation."[28] Psychoanalytic discussion of maternal conflicts, like pop childcare literature, assumes that growing up is essentially the *child's* drama of individuation, played out against and with the mother who is a "given." Similarly in the psychoanalytic reading of witchcraft, the analytic emphasis is not on the witch and her relation to the social so much as on the individual drama of the accuser and recorder—on the ambivalence toward the mother experienced by a host of people who accuse, arraign, search, judge, and finally, condemn a witch. Significantly, that process was then turned to account as narrative or drama, as the lively and sensationalist plays and pamphlet literature witnessed. Magistrates, playwrights and actors, preachers and pamphleteers, the politically ambitious and village hangers-on, all sought or built reputations on the persecution of women as witches.

In a letter to Fliess dated 17 January 1897, Freud observed "that the whole of my brand-new theory of the primary origins of hysteria is already familiar and has been published a hundred times over though several centuries ago."[29] He went on to link witchcraft narratives with "what my patients tell me under psychological treatment" (188). At the end of a later letter in which he elaborated the parallels between witchcraft and his theories of psychosis, Freud added a telling coda: "Being absorbed in all this, I am left cold by the news that the board of professors have proposed my younger colleague in my speciality for the title of professor, thus passing me over, if the news is true" (24 January 1897, 190).

At stake both in Freud's elaboration of the family romance and the labeling of nonconforming women's behavior as hysteria in the nineteenth century, and in prosecuting such women as witches in early modern England, is a struggle for cultural authority. That struggle is witnessed over and over again in Freud's cases and letters as well as in the annals of English witchcraft.

I want to look once more at the discourses of English witchcraft, not for Freud's family romance or the marked maternal body as a psychological configuration, but in yet another context, again keeping in mind Derrida's admonition "that there are only contexts without any center of absolute anchoring."[30] I want to denaturalize the maternal by considering the discovery of witches as an historically specific regime of representation, in which an ideology of the maternal as natural and nurturing, as *presence* in the Derridean sense, is haunted by what it seems to exclude—by writing and representation and the cultural authority they produce, by what I have punningly called "sorciographics."[31]

In early modern England, representation was potentially dangerous and politically charged. As Frances Yates and others have argued, idealized images of Queen Elizabeth were used to consolidate monarchical power: the much-discussed representations, literary and pictorial, of the queen as Eliza, Diana, and the like, or later of James in the court masques. Witchcraft played out the dangers of inverse representation. A common form of proof in witchcraft trials was a clay or waxen image in the likeness of whomever the witch wished to destroy. This frequently recorded witchcraft practice was intended to make the person in whose likeness the image was made become ill and die in slow, dire pain. The sculpting of such an image in the likeness of the monarch was treasonous; such cases were recorded throughout the reigns of Elizabeth and James. In 1580, the Privy Council investigated a mere overheard conversation about a plan to fashion a waxen image of the queen, which would then be destroyed by pins and fire. Interestingly, Holinshed's (1587) account of the death of King Duff, generally said to be among the sources of *Macbeth*, describes such witches' work:

> The king was vexed with no naturall sicknesse, but by sorcerie
> and magicall art, practiced by a sort of witches...[soldiers] break-
> ing into the house, found one of the witches rosting upon a
> wooden broch an image of wax at the fier, resembling in each
> feature the kings person, made and devised (as is to be thought)
> by craft and art of the divell: an other of them sat reciting certa-
> ine words of enchantment...[32]

In the notorious Lancashire trials of 1612, clay pictures and images were frequently adduced as evidence of *maleficium*. Witchcraft involved injury, doing harm; but my emphasis here is on the etymological force of the word, its root in the verb *facio,* to make, construct, fashion, frame, build, erect, produce, compose. The fashioning of such images at once suggests the power and danger of mimesis, of likeness, and the potency and fear surrounding monarchical representation and its potential use in political and social rebellion.[33] As William Perkins declared, quoting scripture in his *Discourse of the Art of Witchcraft* (1616–18), "rebellion is as the sin of witchcraft."

The discovery of witches, as I have argued, is a process of labeling, of reading and interpreting signs. The witch's marks, her behaviors and activities, are not evident and obvious, not *presence,* but depend on reading and interpretation, on writing in the extended sense in which Derrida uses the term in *Grammatology.*[34] Scot closes his *Discovery of Witchcraft* by observing that

> the matter and instruments, wherewith it [witchcraft] is accomplished, are words, charmes, signes, images characters, &: the which words although any other creature doo pronounce, in maner and forme as they doo, leaving out no circumstance requisite or usuall for that action: yet none is said to have the grace or gift to performe the matter, except she be a witch, and so taken, either by hir owne consent, or by others' imputation. (274)

The signs of witchcraft have no intrinsic representational status as such; they were unremarkable except in particular circumstances: words, rhymes, songs, curses; and not only discursive texts but bodily and social texts as well—a doll, a mole, a stray cat entering a door, spoiled beer, a child falling ill. The practice of witchcraft is a semiotic activity that depends on acts of reading, systems of differences.[35] A charm, an incantation, or a blemish has no inherent meaning but comes to mean only in relation to a given speaker and a specific set of circumstances.

In early modern England, rowdy and disorderly women were pitted against authorities who sought control of their representational powers. Accounts sometimes describe witches who spoke in Latin even though they were uneducated peasants.[36] In the earliest recorded Elizabethan case discussed above, Mother Waterhouse made a final confession from the scaffold before her execution. She claimed to have been a witch for twenty-five years and admitted to sending her imps to do harm; but she also told the crowd that she attended church regularly and said her prayers "not in the englyshe and mother tongug" but in Latin, because "Sathan wolde at no tyme suffer her to say it in englysche, but at all tymes in laten" (Haining, 31). Latin prayers were banned during the English Reformation: Mother Waterhouse's witchcraft reads suspiciously like resistance, even rebellion, against the imposition of reformed religion.[37] In his discussion of possession in Renaissance England, Stephen Greenblatt observes that "rivalry among elites competing for the major share of authority was characteristically expressed not only in parliamentary factions but also in bitter struggles over religious doctrine and practice."[38] English witchcraft records suggest that his observation need not be confined to elites. Mother Waterhouse's reluctance to speak the "mother tongue" in prayer, and similar acts by women like her, can be read as a refusal to relinquish charged forms of representation—here Latin—to an emerging secular elite. The continuing resistant practice of Catholicism was labeled "witchcraft" repeatedly during Elizabeth's reign.

Sh. Negot. p 96.

Mother Waterhouse's confession from the scaffold before a crowd dramatizes another feature of this struggle over the means and disposition of representational forms. Catherine Belsey has written eloquently of the dramatic effect of witchcraft trials on the women tried: "The requirement for confessions from the scaffold, so that the people could see how church and state combined to protect them from the enemies of God and society, paradoxically also offered women a place from which to speak in public with a hitherto unimagined authority which was not diminished by the fact that it was demonic."[39] Not only are there frequent references to the crowds at trials and executions as "beholders" or "the audience," as Belsey notes, but also in the numerous witch plays, including *Macbeth* and *The Witch of Edmonton*. Pamphleteers often describe the scene of execution explicitly as a play, and the accounts themselves were cast generically as plays or narratives with the witch in the starring role. In H.F.'s narrative of "A Prodigious & Tragicall History of the Arraignment, Tryall, Confession and Condemnation of six witches at Maidstone in Kent" (1652), not only does the title suggest a drama, but the entire record is presented as a play, with Kent the "scene," "and the beautiful town of Maidstone the stage, whereon this tragicall story was publically acted." Anne Ashby, alias Cobler, "was the chief actresse and...had the greatest part in this tragedy." Women's confessions, and there were many, were a means of self-fashioning, in Greenblatt's continuingly resonant phrase, an opportunity to deploy the powers of representation to which they were often denied access.

In her discussion of the witchcraft trials, Belsey argues that "to speak is to possess meaning, to have access to the language which defines, delimits and locates power. To speak is to become a subject" (191). But to see subjectivity as constituted through speech is problematic: it gives priority to presence and privileges identity; it rehabilitates immediacy, intentionality, and performance. I would locate the contestatory power of witchcraft instead in the *supplement,* the term Derrida appropriates from Rousseau to exemplify contradiction since it connotes both that which supplements what is already complete, and that which supplements what is found lacking and therefore incomplete. The linguistic forms of witchcraft—spells, Latin prayers and phrases, incantations, equivocations—were relegated to the margins yet were paradoxically central to early modern culture.

Equivocation in particular inspired fear in the early modern period precisely because it exposed the fantasy of *presence* at stake in speech, the fantasy that language means what it says and that a given speaker says what she means. At the 1606 trial of Father Garnett, Superior of the Jesuits in England, Sir Edward Coke defined the "doctrine of equivocation" as language "wherein, under the pretext of the lawfulness of a mixt proposition to express one part of a man's mind, and retain another, people are indeed taught, not only simple lying, but fearful and damnable blasphemy."[40] Equivocation is defined by the unsaid, by "mental reservation." An example: the Queen is sought by brigands who, encountering you, ask "Where is the Queen? We are sent to murder her." You cannot tell a lie without offending God, but the truth would make you accessory to the murder of your sovereign. You equivocate by saying, "Nescio [ut te dicam]—I know not [to the end of telling you]." Equivocation enacts the Derridean *supplement;* far from being a bizarre figure alien to "ordinary" language, equivocation is a spectacular and exemplary model of "writing" in the Derridean sense, language that nowhere coincides with speech but advertises its difference from itself. Equivocation seems to have been associated with witches' speech not only in *Macbeth* but in other witchcraft plays and records.[41] In *The Witch of Edmonton,* for example, when the devil enlists Mother Sawyer, she promises, "I am thine, at least so much of me,/As I can call mine own," to which he responds "Equivocations? Art mine or no? speak" (II, i, 139–41).

In his essay "Sending: On Representation" Derrida argues that

> it is only the rendering available of the human subject that
> makes representation happen, and this rendering available is ex-
> actly that which constitutes the subject as a subject. The subject
> is what can or believes it can offer itself representations, dispos-
> ing them and disposing of them. When I say offer itself represen-
> tations, I could just as easily say, scarcely changing context, offer
> itself representatives (political ones for instance) or even offer it-
> self to itself in representation or as a representative.[42]

Subjectivity is not constituted through presence but in repetition, through representation along its entire semantic continuum: as an idea in the mind pointing to the thing; as a picture in place of the thing itself; aesthetic representation—theatrical, poetic, literary or visual; and finally political representation. Derrida plays throughout the essay with the polysemy of the word *representation* and its constitutive force.

Female subjectivity is not constituted through the immediacy of voice, our continuing metaphor even now—from the consciousness-raising of the late 1960s and early 1970s to today's "speak out"—but through and by representation. The feminine speech act is to no avail, has no performative force, if unrecorded. I have tried to read witch-craft precisely not through the maternal body as ground or voice but as a threat posed through representation. Witches threatened hegemonic patriarchal structures precisely not through their bodies but through their representational powers: as cultural producers, as spectacle, as *representatives*—like Margaret, the "libber" of Fife—of an oppositional "femininity." Witchcraft dramatized for its Elizabethan and Jacobean audience, if not for its contemporary readers as well, the spectacle of the production of subjectivity in both senses: the being subject to another and the becoming the subject of discourse. The records of English witchcraft testify not only to the repressive powers of a patriarchal state worked out on the bodies of helpless women; they also testify to another supplementary story. When Agnes Waterhouse cries out from the gallows that she has been a witch these twenty-five years, and gone to church and spoken her prayers in Latin, she comes to occupy through this representation, this equivocal construction of her life, and through my own reading of that representation, a representative's place in our histories.

In his reading of *Othello,* Stanley Cavell calls attention "to the hell and demon staring out of the names of Othello and Desdemona."43 He goes on to suggest, in what he terms "a nearly pure conjecture," the relation of *Othello* to the witch trials of early modern England. His claim hinges on Othello's demand for proof and the trial-like final scenes, but he points out that the play begins with an accusation of witchcraft "and concludes with death as the proof of mortality, that is, of innocence (cf. 'If thou be'st a devil, I cannot kill thee' [V, ii, 287])." But in *Othello,* witchcraft is represented not only as an oppositional femininity but in terms of a racial other as well, and both femininity and blackness are conflated as monstrous.

# FIVE

# "And wash the Ethiop white": Femininity and the Monstrous in Othello

*Shakespear, who is accountable both to the* Eyes *and to the* Ears, *And to convince the very heart of an Audience, shows that* Desdemona *was won by hearing* Othello *talk.... This was the Charm, this was the philtre, the love-powder, that took the Daughter of this Noble Venetian. This was sufficient to make the Black-amoor White, and reconcile all, tho' there had been a Cloven-foot into the bargain.*

Rymer, *"Short View of Tragedy" (1693)*[1]

*It would be something monstrous to conceive this beautiful Venetian girl falling in love with a veritable negro.*

Coleridge, *Lectures and Notes on Shakespeare*[2]

*To a great many people the word "negro" suggests at once the pic-
ture of what they would call a "nigger," the wooly hair, thick lips,
round skull, blunt features, and burnt-cork blackness of the traditional nigger minstrel. Their subconscious generalization is as silly
as that implied in Miss Preston's "the African race" or Coleridge's
"veritable negro." There are more races than one in Africa, and
that a man is black in colour is no reason why he should, even to
European eyes, look sub-human. One of the finest heads I have ever
seen on any human being was that of a negro conductor on an
American Pullman car. He had lips slightly thicker than an ordinary European's, and he had somewhat curly hair; for the rest he
had a long head, a magnificent forehead, a keenly chiselled nose,
rather sunken cheeks, and his expression was grave, dignified, and
a trifle melancholy. He was coalblack, but he might have sat to a
sculptor for a statue of Caesar...*

    M. R. Ridley, editor, the Arden *Othello* (1977)[3]

*M*. R. Ridley's "they" is troublesome. As scholars and teachers,
we use his Arden edition of *Othello* (1958, reprinted 1977)
and find ourselves implicated in his comfortable assumptions about "a
great many people." In answer to the long critical history that sought
to refute Othello's blackness, Ridley affirms that Othello was black,
but he hastens to add an adversative "but." Othello was not a "veritable
negro," he assures us—a type from vaudeville and the minstrel show, a
figure of ridicule unworthy of tragedy who would evidently appear
"sub-human" to European eyes—but a black who looks white and
might have represented the most renowned general of the western
tradition, Caesar. What are we to make of a widely used scholarly edition of Shakespeare, which, in the very act of debunking, canonizes
the prejudices of Rymer and Coleridge?[4] Can we shrug our shoulders,
certain that Ridley's viewpoint represents a long-ago past of American
pullman cars and dignified black conductors? Are such prejudices
dismantled by the most recent reprint, which represents on its cover a

"veritable negro" of exactly the physiognomy Ridley assures us "a great many people" are wrong in imagining?

Much of the disgust Rymer, Coleridge, and other critics betray comes not from the fact of Othello's individual blackness but from the *relation* of that blackness to Desdemona's fair purity. Coleridge calls it "monstrous." Embedded in commentaries on the play that seek to ward off Othello's blackness is the fear of miscegenation, and particularly the white man's fear of the union of black man with white woman. Such commentators occupy the rhetorical position of Roderigo, Brabantio, and Iago, who view the marriage of Othello and Desdemona as against all sense and nature: "I'll refer me to all things of sense,...Whether a maid, so tender, fair, and happy,...Would ever have (to incur a general mock)/Run from her guardage to the sooty bosom/Of such a thing as thou?" (I, ii, 64, 66, 69–71).

In *Othello*, the black Moor and the fair Desdemona are united in a marriage all the other characters view as unthinkable. Shakespeare uses their assumption to generate the plot itself: Iago's ploy to string Roderigo along is his assurance that Desdemona could not, contrary to nature, long love a black man. Even his manipulation of Othello depends on the Moor's own prejudices against his blackness and belief that the fair Desdemona would prefer the white Cassio.

Miscegenation is an issue not only on the level of plot but also of language; for linked oppositions, especially of black and white and their cultural associations, characterize the play's discourse.[5] "Black ram" tups "white ewe"; "fair" Desdemona runs to Othello's "sooty bosom." The Duke mollifies Brabantio with "Your son-in-law is far more fair than black." Desdemona is described, in what for the Renaissance would have been an oxymoron, as a "fair devil" and as "fair paper" and a "goodly book" across the white pages of which Othello fears is written "whore." In the final scene Emilia exclaims in response to Othello's confession that he has killed Desdemona, "O, the more angell she,/And you the blacker devil!" Like the expression "to wash an Ethiop white," Emilia's lines exemplify what I will term rhetorical miscegenation, for despite the semantics of antithesis, the chiasmus allies the opposing terms rhetorically.

In the Renaissance no other colors so clearly implied opposition nor were so frequently used to denote polarization. As Winthrop Jordan points out in his monumental study, *White over Black,* the meaning of *black* even before the sixteenth century, according to the *Oxford English Dictionary,* included "deeply stained with dirt; soiled, dirty, foul; Having dark or deadly purposes, malignant; pertaining to or involving death, deadly, baneful, disastrous, sinister;...iniquitous, atrocious, horribly wicked;...indicating disgrace, censure, liability to punishment, etc."[6] In Jonson's *Masque of Blacknesse,* a preeminent example of the black/white opposition in the period, Stephen Orgel observes that it is "only necessary that the 'twelve *Nymphs, Negro's'* be revealed—that we *see* them—for the 'antimasque' to have taken place."[7] White represented the opposite. In *Othello,* the emphasis on Desdemona's fairness and purity, "that whiter skin of hers than snow/And smooth as monumental alabaster" (V, ii, 4–5), and the idealization of fair female beauty it implies, the entire apparatus of Petrarchanism, is usually said to point up the contrast between Desdemona and Othello. But I want to argue the contrary: femininity is not opposed to blackness and monstrosity, as are the binary opposites black and white, but identified with the monstrous in an identification that makes miscegenation doubly fearful. The play is structured around a cultural aporia, miscegenation.

Femininity interrupts not only the characterological but also the critical discourse of the play. In his commentary, Ridley continues after the passage quoted above: "To give an insult any point and barb it must have some relation to the facts. A woman may call a pale-complexioned rival "pasty" or "whey-faced," but it would be silly to call her swarthy...in the same way, "thick lips" would lose all its venom if it could not be recognizably applicable to Othello's mouth"(lii). Ridley's justification of Othello's blackness and his reading of "thick lips" betray a woefully inadequate sense of irony: literary discourse often works by means of negative example, as in Shakespeare's vaunt "My mistress' eyes are nothing like the sun." But more important than Ridley's limitations as a reader of texts is how he illustrates his point about Othello's blackness: he evokes a cultural prejudice against women, their supposed cattiness in response to a rival. Femininity interrupts Ridley's commentary on Othello's blackness; pitting women

Erasmus ex Luciano.
Abluis Æthiopem frus-
trà: quin desinis arte?
Haud unquà efficies
nox fit ut atra, dies.
Horat. 1. Epist. 10.
Naturam expellas fur-
ca tamen usque re-
curret.

LEAVE of with paine, the blackamore to skowre,
With washinge ofte, and wipinge more then due:
For thou shalt finde, that Nature is of powre,
Doe what thou canste, to keepe his former hue:
Thoughe with a forke, wee Nature thruste awaie,
Shee turnes againe, if wee withdrawe our hande:
And thoughe, wee ofte to conquer her assaie,
Yet all in vaine, shee turnes if still wee stande:
Then euermore, in what thou doest assaie,
Let reason rule, and doe the thinges thou maie.

*——— ——— equusą,*
*Nunquam ex degeneri fiet generosus asello,*
*Et nunquam ex stolido cordatus fiet ab arte.*

Anulus in pict.
poësi.

H           Non

FIGURE SEVEN   Geoffrey Whitney, *A Choice of Emblemes*, H recto (1586).
By permission of the Folger Shakespeare Library.

*"To wash an Ethiop white" is an ancient proverbial expression for impossibil-
ity and bootless labor. Scholars speculate that it originated with Aesop where
the image of scrubbing an Ethiopian is used to demonstrate the power and per-
manence of nature. The expression was common in Greek, and in Latin took
the form "abluis Aethiopem: quid frustra" (you wash an Ethiopian: why the
labor in vain). The emblem reproduced above, from Geoffrey Whitney's widely
circulated emblem book,* A Choice of Emblemes *(Leyden, 1586), moralizes
the adage and emblem in the poem printed beneath the woodcut (fig. 7).*[a]

FIGURE EIGHT  Pear's Soap advertisement (ca. 1875).
From the collection of William G. McLoughlin.

*The expression was proverbial in early modern England and commonplace on
the English and Jacobean stage: in* The White Devil, *for example, the Moor-
ish waiting woman Zanche promises Francisco coin and jewels, a dowry
"should make that sun-burnt proverbe false, /And wash the Ethiop white."* [b]
*By the nineteenth century, the proverb is so familiar that it works as the under-
lying supposition of the popular advertisement reproduced above that paradoxically inverts its meaning. Unlike the sixteenth-century emblem in which
the Ethiop remains black despite the ministrations of the washerwomen, in the
Pear's soap poster (fig. 8), the black baby has been scrubbed almost white. In
the burgeoning consumer culture of the nineteenth century, man-made product promises to reveal beneath black skin a hidden whiteness unimaginable to
early modern man, and its power to do so is authorized by a woman associated with cultural production, the nineteenth-century diva, Adelina Patti. In
the modern period, difference is effaced and whiteness the neutral term: all
men are presumed white regardless of skin color. So on a sign posted outside a
Sussex inn called "The Labour in Vain," two men are represented "hard at
work scrubbing a nigger [sic] till the white should gleam through."* [c]

Notes a, b, and c are to be found on page 161 below.

against women, the critic displaces the struggle of white against black man onto a cultural femininity.

## MISCEGENATION: BLACKS AND THE MONSTROUS

Until the late sixteenth century, speculation about the cause of blackness depended on classical sources rather than experience or observation.[8] In the myth of Phaeton, for example, and Ptolemy's *Tetrabiblos,* Africans' blackness was explained by their proximity to the sun. With the publication in 1589 of the many travel accounts and geographies in Hakluyt's *Principal Navigations,* however, the rehearsal of this ancient topos, though often quoted, was usually countered by the observation that many peoples living equally close to the sun in the Indies and other parts of the New World were of olive complexion and thus disproved the ancients' latitudinal etiology. Myth and empirical observation collided.

In his *Discourse* (1578), George Best, an English traveler, gives an early account of miscegenation and the causes of blackness:

> I my selfe have seene an Ethiopian as blacke as a cole brought into England, who taking a faire English woman to wife, begat a sonne in all respects as blacke as the father was, although England were his native countrey, and an English woman his mother: whereby it seemeth this blacknes proceedeth rather of some natural infection of that man, which was so strong, that neither the nature of the Clime, neither the good complexion of the mother concurring, coulde any thing alter.[9]

Best's account of miscegenation is designed to refute the conventional latitudinal explanation, but it does much more. Not only does it emphasize the contrariety of black and white, "blacke as a cole" and "faire English woman";[10] Best's repetitions also betray the Englishman's ethnocentric preoccupation with his native isle.[11]

Best also proffers an alternative explanation of blackness, which he substitutes for the ancients' geographical theory: "this blacknes proceedeth rather of some natural infection of that man." Best's claim is more radical than his metaphor of disease implies, because to assert that black and white were "naturally" different also posed a theological

CHAPTER FIVE

problem. If the union of black and white always results in black off-spring, "in all respects as blacke as the father," then how can we account for the origin of black or for that matter white, from our first parents? And so Best goes on to explain his claim by referring to scripture and the story in Genesis of Noah and his three sons,

who all three being white, and their wives also, by course of nature should have begotten and brought foorth white children. But the envie of our great and continuall enemie the wicked Spirite is such, that as hee coulde not suffer our olde father Adam to live in the felicitie and Angelike state wherein hee was first created, but tempting him, sought and procured his ruine and fall: so againe, finding at this flood none but a father and three sonnes living, hee so caused one of them to transgresse and disobey his father's commaundement, that after him all his posteritie shoulde bee accursed. The fact of disobedience was this: When Noe at the commandement of God had made the Arke and entered therein. . . hee straitely commaunded his sonnes and their wives, that they. . . should use continencie, and abstaine from carnall copulation with their wives. . . . Which good instructions and exhortations notwithstanding his wicked sonne Cham disobeyed, and being perswaded that the first childe borne after the flood (by right and Lawe of nature) should inherite and possesse all the dominions of the earth, hee contrary to his fathers commaundement while they were yet in the Arke, used company with his wife, and craftily went about thereby to dis-inherite the off-spring of his other two brethren: for the which wicked and detestable fact, as an example for contempt of Almightie God, and disobedience of parents, God would a sonne should bee borne whose name was Chus, who not onely it selfe, but all his posteritie after him should bee so blacke and lothsome, that it might remaine a spectacle of disobedience to all the worlde. And of this blacke and cursed Chus came all these blacke Moores which are in Africa.[12]

Best's myth of a second fall is an extraordinarily rich rehearsal of early English social attitudes. In it are revealed the stock prejudices against blacks in Elizabethan and Jacobean culture: the link between blackness and the devil, the myth of black sexuality, the problem of black subjection to authority, here displaced onto obedience owed to the father and to God. Best's story passes "segregation off as natural—and as the very law of the origin." Derrida's words written about apartheid are suggestive for understanding not only Best's *Discourse* but travel writing more generally: "There's no racism without a language. The point is not that acts of racial violence are only words but rather that they have to have a word. Even though it offers the excuse of blood, color, birth—or, rather, *because* it uses this naturalist and sometimes creationist discourse—racism always betrays the perversion of man, the 'talking animal'."[13]

But Best's account also represents the effects of a specifically Tudor and Stuart economic and social crisis. Noe's son Cham disobeys his father's will because he is ambitious; he seeks to displace his older brothers in the hierarchy of inheritance. Best's account textualizes the problem of social mobility in early modern England; and ironically, given Best's conservatism, it challenges definitions of social identity based on birth. Best betrays a disquieted fear of the social changes taking place in Elizabethan England, of "masterless men" and the challenge to traditional notions of order and degree. At a time when "elite identity gradually came to depend not on inherited or god-given absolute attributes, but on characteristics which could be acquired by human efforts,"[14] Best's account stands in an interesting transitional relation to such changes in the social formation. Cham recognizes the authority of birthright, as does Best's own anxious parenthesis "(by righte and Lawe of nature)," but he seeks to enact the "Lawe of nature" through human effort, an effort duly punished by the ultimate authority, God.

Similarly Best's nationalism and fear of difference are attitudes characteristic of the period. Even by 1578 the English had a considerable material investment in Africa: English explorers had begun to compete with Portuguese traders, and John Hawkins had organized the first successful slave trading venture between Africa and the West Indies in 1563. Best's is not just a fantasy about Africa and blackness but an enabling discourse that sustains a series of material and economic practices and interests. In England by 1596, blacks were numerous enough to generate alarm: Elizabeth wrote to the Lord Mayor of London and to other towns and observed, "there are of late divers blackmoores brought into this realme, of which kinde of people there are allready to manie, consideringe howe God hath blessed this land with great increase of people of our own nation." A week later she observed that "those kinde of people may be well spared in this realme, being so populous" and licensed a certain Casper van Senden, a merchant of Lubeck who had freed eighty-nine Englishmen imprisoned in Spain and Portugal, "to take up so much blackamoores here in this realme and to transport them into Spain and Portugal" for his expenses.[15] Five years later, van Senden was again licensed, this time to deport "the said kind of people...with all speed...out of this her majesty's realms" (January 1601).[16]

Other travel accounts of the period display the intersection between ancient legends and myths about black Africa and contemporary experience, observation, and prejudice. Interspersed with descriptions of African tribal customs, language, and landscape were the legendary stories from Pliny and other classical sources (probably via Mandeville, whose popular *Travels* were included in the 1589 edition of Hakluyt) of the Anthropophagi who wore skins and ate human flesh, of people without heads or speech, of satyrs and Troglodytes who lived in caves and dens.[17] The African landscape was presented descriptively in terms of safe harbors, intense heat, and gigantic waterfalls, but also mythically, as traversed by flames and fire that reached as high as the moon, as ringing with the sound of pipes, trumpets, and drums.[18] Always we find the link between blackness and the monstrous, and particularly a monstrous sexuality. Early travelers describe women held in common and men "furnisht with such members as are after a sort burthensome unto them."[19] These accounts often bore no relation to African sexual habits, but they did confirm earlier discourses and representations of African sexuality found in Herodotus, Diodorus, and other classical authors.

The prejudices of the ancients were preserved into the fifteenth and sixteenth centuries. Early cartographers ornamented maps with representations of naked black men bearing enormous sexual organs. Leo Africanus's *Historie of Africa* (1526), widely available in Latin in England and translated in 1600 by John Pory, claimed "negros" were "prone to Venery." In Jean Bodin's widely read work of political philosophy *The Six Bookes of a Commonweale* he argues against slavery but nevertheless betrays the conventional prejudice about black sexuality when he claims, "there be in mans bodie some members, I may not call them filthie (for that nothing can so be which is naturall) but yet so shamefull, as that no man except he be past all shame, can without blushing reveale or discover the same: and doe they [blacks] for that cease to be members of the whole bodie?"[20] Because of his organic conception of the state, Bodin's political theory does not permit a dualism, slavery for some, freedom for others. But he is so shamed by those members, and the Africans custom of exposing them, he dresses his prose in a series of parentheses and clauses that effectively obscure its meaning.

Such attitudes, both inherited from the past and reconstructed by contemporary historiographers, humanists, and travelers, were quickly assimilated into the drama and culture of early modern England.[21] In *Titus Andronicus,* for example, the lustful union of Aaron and Tamor resulted in a black baby called "a devil" in the play. Similarly, Volpone's copulations that result in monstrous offspring—the fool, dwarf, and hermaphrodite—are accomplished with "beggars, gipseys and Jewes, and black moores." In Bacon's *New Atlantis* (1624), a holy hermit "desired to see the Spirit of Fornication; and there appeared to him a foul little Aethiop." Treatises on witchcraft and trials of the period often reported that the devil appeared to the possessed as a black man.[22] Finally, contemporary ballads and broadsides, the Renaissance equivalent of news stories, popularized monstrous births such as one recorded by the Stationers' Register (1580): a monstrous child, born at Fenstanton in Huntingdonshire, was described as "a monster with a black face, the Mouth and Eyes like a Lyon which was both Male and Female."[23]

MONSTROUS DESIRE IN *OTHELLO*

In *Renaissance Self-Fashioning,* Stephen Greenblatt has argued persuasively that Othello submits to narrative self-fashioning, his own and Iago's. He demonstrates the congruence between their narratives and the ideological narratives of Renaissance culture—most powerfully, the orthodox Christian attitude toward sexuality. Iago and Othello, he observes, are linked by shared, if dialectically opposed, cultural values about women and sexuality. Greenblatt quotes Kenneth Burke's claim that they are "consubstantial":

> Iago, to arouse Othello, must talk a language that Othello knows as well as he, a language implicit in the nature of Othello's love as the idealization of his private property in Desdemona. This language is the dialectical opposite of Othello's; but it so thoroughly shares a common ground with Othello's language that its insinuations are never for one moment irrelevant to Othello's thinking. Iago must be cautious in leading Othello to believe them as true: but Othello never for a moment doubts them as *values*.[24]

For Greenblatt, Othello's "identity depends upon a constant performance, as we have seen, of his story, a loss of his own origins, an embrace and perpetual reiteration of the norms of another culture."[25]

What are Othello's lost origins? Greenblatt implies as somehow anterior to identity-as-performance an essential self, an ontological subjectivity, an Edenic moment of black identity prior to discourse, outside, in Derrida's phrase quoted earlier, "the perversion of man, the 'talking animal'." Derrida's words about racism are pertinent to a discussion of origins as well and permit the substitution of ontology for race: "there are no origins without a language." Othello doesn't lose "his own origins"; his only access to those "origins" are the exotic ascriptions of European colonial discourse. Othello's stories of slavery and adventure are *precisely* a rehearsal of his origins, from his exotic tales of monstrous races to the story of the handkerchief's genealogy in witchcraft and sibylline prophecy. Othello charms by reiterating his origins even as he submits and embraces the dominant values of Venetian culture. His successful courtship of Desdemona suggests that those origins are not simply repressive but also enabling. Greenblatt is moving in his representation of Othello's submission to such cultural plots, but by focusing on Othello's ideological complicity, Greenblatt effectively erases the other that is constituted discursively in the play as both woman and black. Othello is both a speaking subject, a kind of

George Best recounting his tales of conquest, and at the same time the object of his "traveler's history" by virtue of his blackness, which originates with the very monstrous races he describes.[26]

Similarly he is both the representative and upholder of a rigorous sexual code that prohibits desire and defines it even within marriage as adulterous, as Greenblatt claims, and yet also the sign of a different, unbridled sexuality. Greenblatt effaces the profound paradox of the black Othello's embrace of Christian sexual mores: Othello is both monster and hero, and his own sexuality is appropriately indecipherable.[27] As champion of Christian cultural codes, he assures the senators his wish to take his bride with him to Cyprus is not "to please the palate of my appetite,/Nor to comply with heat, the young affects/In my defunct, and proper satisfaction" (I, iii, 262–64). He loves Desdemona "but to be free and bounteous of her mind" (265). Like Brabantio, Iago, and Roderigo, Othello perceives of his love and indeed his human—as opposed to bestial—identity as depending on property rights, on absolute ownership:

> O curse of marriage,
> That we can call these delicate creatures ours,
> And not their appetites! I had rather be a toad,
> And live upon the vapour in a dungeon,
> Than keep a corner in a thing I love,
> For others' uses.
>
> (III, iii, 271–76)

But opposed to the representation of Othello's participation in the play's dominant sex/gender system is a conventional representation of black sexuality evoked by other characters and by Othello himself in his traveler's tales and through his passionate action. The textual allusions to bestiality, lubricity, and the demonic have been often noted. Iago rouses Brabantio with "an old black ram/Is tupping your white ewe...the devil will make a grandsire of you" (I, i, 88–89, 91), and "you'll have your daughter cover'd with a Barbary horse; you'll have your nephews neigh to you; you'll have coursers for cousins, and gennets for germans" (110–13). "Your daughter and the Moor, are now making the beast with two backs" (115–16); and Desdemona is transported, according to Roderigo, "to the gross clasps of a lascivious

Moor" (I, i, 126). Not until the third scene is the Moor named, and the delay undoubtedly dramatizes Othello's blackness and the audience's shared prejudices vividly conjured up by Iago's pictorial visions of carnal knowledge. To read Othello as congruent with the attitudes toward sexuality and femininity expressed in the play by the Venetians, Iago, Brabantio, Roderigo, and Cassio—and opposed to Desdemona's desire—is to ignore the threatening sexuality of the other, which divides the representation of Othello's character.[28] Othello internalizes alien cultural values, but the otherness that divides him from that culture and links him to the play's other marginality, femininity, remains in visual and verbal allusion.

For the white male characters of the play, the black man's power resides in his sexual difference. Their preoccupation with black sexuality is not the eruption of a normally repressed animal sexuality in the "civilized" white male but of the feared power and potency of a different and monstrous sexuality, which threatens the white male sexual norm represented in the play most emphatically by Iago. For however evil Iago reveals himself to be, as Spivak pointed out, like the Vice in the medieval morality—or we could add, the trickster-slave of Latin comedy—Iago enjoys a privileged relation with the audience.[29] He possesses what can be termed the discourse of knowledge in *Othello* and annexes not only the other characters but the resisting spectator as well into his world and its perspective. By virtue of his manipulative power and his superior knowledge and control over the action, which we share, we are implicated in his machinations and the cultural values they imply.[30] Iago is a cultural hyperbole; he does not oppose cultural norms so much as hyperbolize them.[31]

Before the English had wide experience of miscegenation, they seem to have believed, as George Best recounts, that the black man had the power to subjugate his partner's whiteness, to make both his "victim" and her offspring resemble him, by making them both black—a literal blackness in the case of a child, a metaphorical blackness in the case of a sexual partner. So in *Othello* Desdemona becomes "thou black weed" (IV, iii, 69), and the white pages of her "goodly book" are blackened by writing when Othello imagines "whore" inscribed across them. At IV, iii, she explicitly identifies herself with her mother's maid Barbary, whose name indicates blackness. The union of

Desdemona and Othello represents a sympathetic identification between femininity and the monstrous that offers a potentially subversive recognition of sexual and racial difference.[32]

Both the male-dominated Venetian world of *Othello* and the criticism the play has generated have been dominated by a scopic economy that privileges sight, from the spectacular opposition of black and white to Othello's demands for ocular proof of Desdemona's infidelity. But Desdemona *hears* Othello and loves him, awed by his traveler's tales of the dangers he had endured, dangers that emphasize his link with monsters and marvels. Her responses to his tales are perceived as voracious: she "devours" his speech with a "greedy ear," a conflation of the oral and aural; and his language betrays a masculine fear of a cultural femininity envisioned as a greedy insatiable mouth, always seeking increase—a point of view reinforced by Desdemona's response to their reunion at Cyprus.[33] Desdemona is presented in the play as a sexual subject who hears and desires, and that desire is punished because the nonspecular, or nonphallic, sexuality it displays is frightening and dangerous.[34] Instead of a specular imaginary, Desdemona's desire is represented in terms of an aural-oral libidinal economy that generates anxiety in Othello, as his account to the Senate of his courtship via fiction betrays.[35] Othello fears Desdemona's desire because it invokes his monstrous difference from the sex/race code he has adopted and implicates him in femininity, allying him with witchcraft and an imagined monstrous sexual appetite.

Thomas Rymer, a kind of critical Iago, claims the moral of *Othello* is first, "a caution to all Maidens of Quality how, without their parents consent, they run away with Blackamoors," an instruction he follows with the Italian source's version: "Di non si accompagnare con huomo cui la natura & il cielo & il modo della vita disgiunge da noi."[36] Both Rymer and Cinthio reveal how Desdemona is punished for her desire: she hears Othello and desires him, and is punished because she threatens a white male hegemony in which women cannot be desiring subjects. When Desdemona comes to tell her version of their wooing, she says: "I saw Othello's visage in his mind." The allusion here is certainly to her audience's prejudice against the black "visage" both the senators and Shakespeare's audience see in *Othello,* but Desdemona "saw" his visage by hearing the tales he tells of his past, tales that, far from washing the Moor white as her line seems to imply, emphatically affirm Othello's link with Africa and its legendary monstrous creatures. Rymer's moral points up the patriarchal and scopic assumptions of his culture that are assumed as well in the play and most pointedly summed up by Brabantio's often quoted lines: "Look to her, Moor, have a quick eye to see:/She has deceiv'd her father, may do thee" (I, iii, 292–93). Fathers have the right to dispose of their daughters as they see fit, to whom they see fit; and disobedience against the father's law is merely a prelude to the descent into hell and blackness the play enacts—a fall, we might recall, Best's tale uncannily predicts. Desdemona's desire threatens the patriarchal privilege of disposing daughters, and in the play world it signals sexual duplicity and lust.

The irony, of course, is that Othello himself is the instrument of punishment. He enacts the moral Rymer and Cinthio point, both confirming cultural prejudice by his monstrous murder of Desdemona and punishing her desire that transgresses the norms of the Elizabethan sex/race system. Both Othello and Desdemona deviate from the norms of the sex/race system in which they participate from the margins.[37] Othello is not, in Cinthio's words, "da noi," one of "us," nor is Desdemona. Women depend for their class status on their affiliation with men—fathers, husbands, sons—and Desdemona forfeits that status and the protection it affords when she marries outside the categories her culture allows. For her transgression, her desire of difference, she is punished not only by a loss of status but even of life. The woman's desire is punished, and ultimately its monstrous inspiration as well. As the object of Desdemona's illegitimate passion, Othello both figures monstrosity and femininity *and* at the same time represents the white male norms the play encodes through Iago, Roderigo, and Brabantio.[38] Not surprisingly, Othello reveals at last a complicitous self-loathing, for blackness is as loathsome to him as to George Best, or any male character in the play, or ostensibly the audience.

At IV, i, Iago constructs a drama in which Othello is instructed to interpret a scene rich in its figurations of desire and the monstrous. Cast as eavesdropper and voyeur by Iago, Othello imagines and thus constitutes a sexual encounter and pleasure that excludes him and a Desdemona as whore instead of fair angel. Cassio's mocking rehearsal of Bianca's love is not the sight/site of Desdemona's transgression, as Othello believes, but its representation; ironically this theatrical representation directed by Iago functions as effectively as would the real. Representation for Othello is transparent. The male gaze is privileged; it constructs a world that the drama plays out. The aptly and ironically named Bianca is a cypher for Desdemona whose "blackened whiteness" she embodies. Plots of desire conventionally figure woman as the erotic object, but in *Othello* the iconic center of the spectacle is shifted from the woman to the monstrous Othello, whose blackness charms *and* threatens but ultimately fulfills the cultural prejudices it represents. Othello is both hero and outsider because he embodies not only the norms of male power and privilege represented by the white male hegemony ruling Venice, a world of prejudice, ambition, jealousy, and the denial of difference, but also the threatening power of the alien: Othello is a monster in the Renaissance sense of the word, a deformed creature like the hermaphrodites and other strange spectacles so fascinating to the early modern period. And *monstrum,* the word itself, figures both the creature and its movement into representation, for it meant as well a showing or demonstration, a *representation.*

## HISTORICAL CONTINGENCY: REREADING *OTHELLO*

*The position which a text occupies within the ideological relations of class struggle at its originating moment of production is...no necessary indication of the positions which it may subsequently come to occupy in different historical and political contexts.*

Tony Bennett, *"Text and History"*[39]

*His nose was rising and* Roman, *instead of* African *and flat: His Mouth the finest shaped that could be seen; far from those great turn'd Lips, which are so natural to the rest of the Negroes. The whole Proportion and air of his face was so nobly and exactly form'd, that bating his colour, there could be nothing in Nature more beautiful, agreeable and handsome.*

Aphra Behn, *Oroonoko (1688)*[40]

CHAPTER FIVE

Behn's description of her black protagonist Oroonoko is startling in its congruence with Ridley's portrait of the black Othello with which we began. A black tragic hero of Othello's proportions, or Behn's noble Oroonoko, is only possible if black is really white, if features are "classical"—that is, European—and color is merely an unfortunate accident. By the late seventeenth century, the role and status of blacks in English society has changed, and the discourse of racism is fully established. No longer "spectacles of strangeness" and monstrosity who occupied unstable, exotic, and mythic ideological roles, they were now slaves, situated in a growing capitalist economy, which their exploited labor sustained. In the sixteenth and early seventeenth centuries, the slave trade in England had been desultory and the status of blacks liminal rather than fixed. As Best's *Discourse* and the accounts of early voyagers illustrate, blacks occupied mythic roles rather than positions as mere chattel or economic linchpins. In Elizabethan and Jacobean England, blacks were not only servants; they owned property, payed taxes, and went to church.[41] But with the establishment of the sugar industry in the Caribbean and the tobacco and cotton industries in America, the position of blacks changed, and their value as slave labor was fully recognized and exploited. The Royal African Company, chartered in 1672, monopolized the African trade until 1698 when the expansion of the colonies dependent on slave labor was so great that it was deprived of its exclusive rights and the market opened to competition. Newspapers of the late seventeenth century testify to a changed view of blacks, with advertisements of slaves for sale and, more importantly, Hue and Cry notices seeking runaways often described as wearing collars emblazoned with their owner's arms or with inscriptions such as one reported in *The London Gazette* (1688): "The Lady Bromfield's black, in Lincoln's Inn Fields."

By the late seventeenth century, Englishmen had come to recognize the significance of the slave trade to the British economy. In 1746 Postlethwayt put that recognition forcefully into words: "The most approved Judges of the commercial Interests of these Kingdoms have ever been of Opinion, that our West-Indian and African trades are the most nationally beneficial of any we carry on...and the daily Bread of the most considerable Part of our British Manufacturers, [is] owing primarily to the Labour of Negroes."[42] By the mid-eighteenth century, the *Gentleman's Magazine* claimed there were some twenty thousand blacks in London. Their increasing numbers led to growing prejudice and fear that they threatened the position of white working people. In pamphlets and the popular press, blacks were represented increasingly in caricatures as bestial, ape-like, inhuman, and stripped of the exotic or mythic dimensions that characterized sixteenth- and early seventeenth-century discourse.

By the time of Rymer's attack on *Othello,* Shakespeare's heroic and tragic representation of a black man seemed unthinkable. In his "Short View of Tragedy," (1693), Rymer found Shakespeare's choice reprehensible, a transgression both of tragic and social decorum.[43] Rymer's attitude toward the "blackmoor" is historically predictable; more surprising, perhaps, is his critical slippage, like Ridley's some two hundred and fifty years later, from blackness to femininity.[44]

In ridiculing *Othello,* Rymer notoriously claimed that the play's moral was "a warning to all good Wives that they look well to their Linnen."[45] He devotes the last pages of his sardonic attack to the "Tragedy of the Handkerchief," claiming that "had it been Desdemona's Garter, the Sagacious Moor might have smelt a Rat; but the handkerchief is so remote a trifle, no Booby on this side of *Mauritania* cou'd make any consequence from it....Yet we find it entered into our Poets head to make a Tragedy of this *Trifle.*"[46] Rymer takes issue with Shakespeare's presentation of the handkerchief because he finds it too trifling a detail to sustain tragedy. His comment here reflects not only the changed generic expectations of neoclassicism but also Rymer's cultural prejudices against women, their supposed materiality and preoccupation with the trivial.[47] In the early modern period, the handkerchief was in fact a sign of wealth and status; by the early eighteenth century, however, it had become commonplace.[48] In cinquecento Venice, possession of a lady's handkerchief was considered proof of adultery and led to stringent punishments. In 1416, for example, a certain Tomaso Querini received a stiff sentence of eighteen months in jail and a fine of five hundred lire di piccoli for carrying out "many dishonesties" with Maria, wife of Roberto Bono. Records from the time describe Tomaso's crime as having "presumed to follow the said lady and on this public street took from her hands a handkerchief, carrying it off with him. As a result of this deed the said Tomaso entered the home of Roberto many times during the day and night and committed many dishonesties with this lady with the highest dishonor for ser Roberto."[49]

Many critics and readers of the play have sought to save Shakespeare's handkerchief from Rymer's harsh judgment by demonstrating not its historical significance as a sign of adultery but its symbolic significance and meaning. Their efforts have been limited by their own historical boundaries and by reigning critical preoccupations and practices that too often seek to work out equations that restrict the richness of handkerchief as signifier. The handkerchief in *Othello* is what we might term a snowballing signifier, for, as it passes from hand to hand, both literal and critical, it accumulates myriad associations and meanings.[50] It first appears simply as a love token given by Othello to Desdemona and therefore treasured by her; only later do we learn the details of its provenance and design. In the Renaissance, strawberries signified virtue and goodness, but also hypocritical virtue as symbolized by the frequently occuring design and emblem of a strawberry plant with an adder hiding beneath its leaves.[51] This doubleness is, of course, appropriate for Othello's perception of Desdemona; for when the handkerchief is first given, it represents her virtue and their chaste love, but it later becomes a sign, indeed a proof, of her unfaithfulness. Iago's description of the napkin as "spotted" constitutes a new meaning for Othello: the strawberries become signs of Desdemona's deceit.[52]

In psychoanalytic terms, the handkerchief Othello inherits from his mother and then gives to Desdemona has been read symptomatically as the fetishist's substitution for the mother's missing phallus. Like the shoe Freud's young boy substitutes "for the woman's (mother's) phallus which the little boy once believed in and does not wish to forego," the handkerchief is the fetish that endows "women with the attribute which makes them acceptable as sexual objects"— that is, makes them like men.[53] For Othello, it both conceals and reveals Desdemona's imperfection, her lack. But the psychoanalytic scenario is problematic because it privileges a male scopic drama, casting the woman as other, as a failed man, thereby effacing her difference and concealing her sexual specificity behind the fetish. The handkerchief in *Othello* does indeed figure a lack, but ironically it figures not simply the missing penis but the lack around which the play's dramatic action is structured, a feminine desire that is described in the play as aberrant and "monstrous" or a "monster."[54] The handkerchief, associated with the mother, witchcraft, and the marvelous, represents the link between femininity and the monstrous, which Othello and Desdemona's union figures in the play. It figures a female sexual topography that is more than a sign of male possession, violated virginity, or even deceit, and more than the fetishist's beloved object. It figures not only Desdemona's lack, as in the traditional psychoanalytic reading, but also her own sexual parts: the nipples,—sometimes, incidentally, represented in the courtly love *blason* as strawberries— lips, and even perhaps, the clitoris, the berry of sexual pleasure nestled within its flanged leaves.[55]

The handkerchief, therefore, is significant not only historically, as an indicator of class and/or transgression, and psychologically, because it signifies male fears of duplicity, consummation, and castration, but also politically, precisely because it has become a *feminine* trifle. *Othello*'s tragic action is structured not around an heroic act or even object—a battle as in *Antony and Cleopatra* or kingship as in *Macbeth* and *King Lear*—but around a trifle, a feminine toy. Instead of relegating *Othello* to the critical category of domestic tragedy, always implicitly or explicitly pejorative because of its focus on woman, jealousy, and a triangle, we can reread *Othello* from another perspective, also admittedly historically bound, that seeks to displace conventional interpretations by exposing the extraordinary fascination and fear of racial and sexual difference in Elizabethan and Jacobean culture. Desdemona and Othello, woman and black man, are represented by discourses about femininity and blackness that managed and produced difference in early modern England.

## COLONIALISM AND SEXUAL DIFFERENCE

Was Shakespeare a racist who condoned the negative image of blacks in his culture? Is Desdemona somehow guilty in her stubborn defense of Cassio and her admiring remark "Ludovico is a proper man."[56] Or guilty in a newer critical vocabulary, in her "erotic submission, [which,] conjoined with Iago's murderous cunning, far more effectively, if unintentionally, subverts her husband's carefully fashioned identity."[57] Readers preoccupied with formal dramatic features claim such questions are moot, that the questions themselves expose the limits of moral or political readings of texts because they raise the spectres of intention or ignore art's touted transcendence of history. But as much recent poststructuralist and/or political criticism has demonstrated, even highly formalist readings are political, inscribed in the discourse both of the period in which the work was produced and that in which it is consumed.

The task of a political criticism is not merely to expose or demystify the ideological discourses that organize literary texts but to *reconstitute* those texts, to reread canonical texts in noncanonical ways that reveal the contingency of so-called canonical readings, that disturb conventional interpretations and discover them as partisan, constructed, made rather than given, natural and inevitable. Such strategies of reading are particularly necessary in drama because the dramatic immediacy of theatrical representation obscures the fact that the audience is watching a highly artificial enactment—in the case of *Othello*, of what a non-African and a man has made into a vision of blackness and femininity, of passion and desire in the other, the marginal, outside culture yet simultaneously within it.

Shakespeare was certainly subject to the racist, sexist, and colonialist discourses of his time; but by making the black Othello a hero, and by making Desdemona's love for Othello and her transgression of her society's norms for women in choosing him sympathetic, Shakespeare's play stands in a contestatory relation to the hegemonic ideologies of race and gender in early modern England. Othello is, of course, the play's hero only within the terms of a white, elitist male ethos, and he suffers the generic "punishment" of tragedy; but he is nevertheless represented as heroic and tragic at an historical moment when the only role blacks played onstage was that of a villain of low status. The case of Desdemona is more complex because the fate she suffers is the conventional fate assigned to the desiring woman. Nevertheless, Shakespeare's representation of her as at once virtuous and desiring, and of her choice in love as heroic rather than demonic, dislocates the conventional ideology of gender the play also enacts.

# SIX

# Englishing the Other: "le tiers exclu" and Shakespeare's Henry V

*A*t his departure in search of a northwest passage, the English explorer Martin Frobisher was exhorted by Queen Elizabeth to bring back some of the native peoples he encountered on his voyage. Elizabeth betrayed her characteristic ambivalence toward colonial enterprise: she desired to see the "spectacle of strangeness" but at the same time ordered Frobisher not to compel the Indians against their wills. In his account of the voyage (1577), Frobisher reveals that despite Elizabeth's warning he laid hold of his captive forcibly. Worried about the well-being of his "strange and new prey," he also took a woman captive for his prisoner's comfort. Here is the account of that meeting:

> At their first encountring they beheld each the other very wistly a good space, without speech or word uttered, with great change of colour and countenance, as though it seemed the griefe and disdeine of their captivity had taken away the use of their tongues and utterance: the woman at the first very suddenly, as though she disdeined or regarded not the man, turned away, and began to sing as though she minded another matter: but being againe brought together, the man brake up the silence first, and with sterne and stayed countenance, began to tell a long solemne tale to the woman, whereunto she gave good hearing, and interrupted him nothing, till he had finished, and afterwards, being growen into more familiar acquaintance by speech, they were turned together, so that (I thinke) the one would hardly have lived without the comfort of the other. And for so much as we could perceive, albeit they lived continually together, yet they did never use as man & wife, though the woman spared not to doe all necessary things that appertained to a good houswife indifferently for them both, as in making cleane their Cabin, and every other thing that appertained to his ease: for when he was seasicke, she would make him cleane, she would kill and flea the dogs for their eating, and dresse his meate. Only I thinke it worth the noting the continencie of them both: for the man would never shift himselfe, except he had first caused the woman to depart out of his cabin, and they

both were most shamefast, least any of their privie parts should be discovered, either of themselves, or any other body.[1]

This remarkable description of the Eskimos' domestic relations is of interest as much for what it reveals about the captors as for its description of the Eskimos themselves. The English found the Eskimos particularly troubling because they were both savage and civilized: they wore sewn leather clothing, unlike their southern counterparts; they "dressed" their meat, that is, prepared and cooked it; their complexions were as white as those of many Englishmen. But they were also savage: they sometimes ate raw flesh washed down, according to contemporary observers, with ox blood; they lived underground in caves or burrows with holes for doors; they were nomads, "a dispersed and wandering nation...without any certaine abode." Frobisher's account demonstrates the English attitude; he and his men watch their captives as if they were animals in a cage.

But Frobisher not only constructs the alien; he fashions the Eskimos into an English man and wife. She is chaste, silent, and obedient, blushing modestly at first sight of her fellow, listening in silence to him speak, a good housewife in attending to "house" and "husband." Frobisher marks the man as speaking first, in monologue, "with sterne and stayed countenance," sublating the woman's initiative in breaking silence with her phatic singing. The man is comically helpless, almost pompous; the woman cares for him in sickness and prepares his food. Both show what for the English sailors seems a surprising sexual continence and modesty: Frobisher is amazed that being "turned together...they did never use as man & wife" and betrays his incredulity with expressions of doubt—the qualifying "I think" and "for so much as we could perceive." However willing the English are to see the strangeness of Eskimo customs—domiciliary, dietary, sartorial—heterosexual relations are always the same. For the English explorer, gender—and particularly womanhood—is a given of nature rather than a construct of culture; it is transhistorical and transnational, to be encountered by Englishmen in their colonial travels the world over.

In Frobisher's account, ethnography is domesticated: he constructs the Eskimos' relations as an English marriage—domestic, naturalized, immanent. In doing so, he suppresses the Eskimos' strangeness not only for the Elizabethans but for modern readers of Renaissance texts as well, and thereby obscures the contingency of gender and sexuality. In his brilliant analysis of Renaissance culture and its response to the other, "Strange Things, Gross Terms, Curious Customs: The Rehearsal of Cultures in the Late Renaissance," Steven Mullaney casually remarks that Frobisher "brought an Eskimo couple back from his second voyage," though Frobisher's own account makes the status of the two Eskimos' relation perfectly clear.[2] Mullaney observes that "difference draws us to it; it promises pleasure and serves as an invitation to firsthand experience, otherwise known as colonization." But as Mullaney's elision of the Eskimos' relation suggests, the pleasures of sexual difference invite essentialist assumptions about gender and heterosexuality.

The early modern English fascination with the strange and alien has been widely documented. Explorers who returned from their voyages with native peoples often turned their captives to account, as Stephano and Trinculo plan to do with Caliban. Ostensibly brought back to be Christianized and to learn English language and customs so as to return one day to "civilize" their fellows, new world peoples were displayed like freaks and wild animals for viewers willing to pay a few pence for the sight. Ballads, almanacs, pamphlets, travelogues, and plays record not only the English interest in the other but the conflation of various discourses of difference—gender, race, class or degree, the nation state—in representations of difference. In *Tamar Cam* (1592), for example, there is an entry of "Tartars, Geates, Amozins, Negars, ollive cullord moores, Canniballs, Hermaphrodites, Pigmes," a series that witnesses how the English set themselves off from their many others—sexual, racial, social. English culture defined itself in opposition to exotic others represented as monstrous but also in opposition to its near neighbors on which it had expansionist aims, the Welsh, the Irish, the Scots. As Mullaney observes, "learning strange tongues or collecting strange things, rehearsing the words and ways of marginal or alien cultures, upholding idleness for a while—these are the activities of a culture in the process of extending its boundaries and reformulating itself."[3]

That extension of boundaries is often represented in drama linguistically, and nowhere more than in Shakespeare's *Henry V.* M.C. Bradbrook, C. L. Barber, Robert Weimann, and Steven Mullaney, Shakespeareans who approach the plays from widely varied perspectives, have all demonstrated how Shakespeare's language and stagecraft preserved or consumed the customs and voices of other cultures. The play is notable for what Bakhtin has called *heteroglossia,* its various voices or linguistic sociality.[4] According to Bakhtin, language is stratified not only into dialects in the linguistic sense but also "into languages that are socio-ideological: languages of social groups, 'professional' and 'generic' languages, languages of generations and so forth."[5]

Unlike the earlier plays in the tetralogy, the social voices of *Henry V* are not represented only in the taverns but on the battlefield and in the palace. Its wealth of dialects, its proverbs and folk sayings, are in the mouths not only of Bardolph, Pistol, and the Hostess but of respected soldiers of the "middling sort," and even the elite, as in the contest of proverbs between Orleans and the Constable of France. The linguist M. A. K. Halliday's distinction between dialect (language determined by who you are, your socioregional origins) and what he terms register (language determined by use and expressing the social division of labor) provides a useful schema for analyzing the way in which the play represents both social and gender difference linguistically.[6]

According to Halliday, register is affected by a number of variables including role relationships, social situations, and symbolic and ideological organization. Henry moves among a variety of speakers, situations and modes of speech; he can vary his linguistic register according to context. Whereas the soldiers are limited by their dialects and by sociolects of degree, Henry is represented by a flexible linguistic register: he speaks with the voice of monarchical authority and the elite at one moment, with the voice of a common soldier at another. With his bishops, his nobles, and the French he speaks a highly rhetorical verse that indicates his status as king and is marked by mythological and scriptural allusion, the royal "we," the synecdochic figuration of the king's two bodies, and references to his genealogy and elite pastimes. With his soldiers on the field he speaks in another register, a prose of mercantile allusion, proverbial and colloquial.

Henry's linguistic flexibility and virtuosity enables him, unlike the other characters of the play, to move among and seemingly *to master* varied social groups. That seeming mastery is perhaps nowhere more prominent than in those speeches in which the king presents himself as constrained by "ceremony" rather than empowered by "place, degree, and form" and their appropriate rhetorics.[7] Paradoxically, perhaps, Henry's self-conscious manipulation of linguistic register is in part what undermines the play's glorification of the monarch and has prompted recent ironic readings.[8]

A dialectical speaker is quite different; his language limits his status, role and mobility. Fluellen, MacMorris, and Jamy all demonstrate not simply the variety of Englishmen on the battlefield at Agincourt and their unity under Henry, as has so often been noted, but speech and behavior governed by socioregional variables. An early modern illustration of the kind of linguistic determinism Halliday posits would be the annexation of Wales in 1536 that "permitted only English speakers to hold administrative office."[9] The non-elite, then, are presented as linguistically disadvantaged by dialect or, in the case of Princess Katherine, excluded from English altogether by her mother tongue.

The English lesson between the Princess and Alice at III, iv, the only scene in the play that takes place in a private, domestic space, powerfully represents Katherine's linguistic disadvantage. The dialogue locates and confines her not even to the comprehensible if comic dialect of the mother tongue spoken by the captains and soldiers but to a strange disfigured tongue and body. It is preceded by Henry's speech before the walls of Harfleur, often described as a generalized "disquietingly excessive evocation of suffering and violence," but in fact suffering and violence rhetorically enacted on the aged, the helpless, and especially on women—their bodies, the products of their bodies, and the ideological positions they occupy in the family and the commonwealth.[10] In these notorious lines, the expansionist aims of the nation state are worked out on and through the woman's body. Henry speaks to the men of Harfleur by means of transactions in women: violation and the rape of "fair, fresh virgins" and the slaying of mothers' "flow'ring infants." The speech ends with a vision of familial destruction:

look to see

The blind and bloody soldier with foul hand
[Desire] the locks of your shrill-shrieking daughters;
Your fathers taken by the silver beards,
And their most reverend heads dash'd to the walls;
Your naked infants spitted upon pikes,
Whiles the mad mothers with their howls confus'd
Do break the clouds, as did the wives of Jewry
At Herod's bloody-hunting slaughtermen.

(III, iii, 33–41)[11]

In Henry's speech, the power of the English army is figured as aggressive violence against the weak, and particularly as sexual violence against women. In the dialogue between Katherine and Alice that follows, the "English" also conquer the woman's body. The bawdy of the lesson, the Princess's helpless rehearsal of gross terms, as Steven Mullaney calls it, confines woman discursively to the sexual sphere.[12] The "lesson" moves from sexually unmarked, if potentially eroticized, parts—the hand, fingers, nails, neck, elbow, chin—to sexually specific puns that name the sexual act and women's genitals. Katherine is dispersed or fragmented not through a visual description of her body as spectacle, as in the *blason* and its variants in Renaissance love poetry, but through an o/aural wordplay that dismembers her. Nancy Vickers suggests that this synecdochic mode of representing woman as a fragmented body was disseminated in Petrarch's *Rime Sparse*.[13] She outlines a history of such modes of representing woman and her body, from Latin love elegy to the novel and contemporary film. The most powerful theorization of this mode of representation has been articulated in contemporary film theory describing a fetishized female body, scattered, fragmented, and mastered—by a male gaze.[14] In drama, which lacks the mastering perspective of the look (cinematic or authorial), spoken language—and particularly the variable register—becomes the means of mastery, a linguistic command imposed not on, as in cinema or in Petrarch, "the silent image of woman still tied to her place as bearer of meaning" but on woman as speaker. The dialogue at III, iv, literally "Englishes"

Katherine and her body, constituting her as a sexual object that, as the final scene demonstrates, will be disposed of in a sexual exchange, another form of communication that binds men to men, England to France.

The sexual exchange at Act V is framed by Burgundy's speech representing France as a rank, wild, and overgrown garden (V, ii, 23–67. Peace, personified as a poor, naked woman has been chased from "our fertile France," and through a slippage in pronouns, France itself is feminized, a fitting figure for the following courtship scene resulting in the marriage of "England and fair France." Henry tells Burgundy quite clearly that "you must buy that Peace/With full accord to all our just demands" (V, ii, 70–71). Though most modern editions shift to lower case in Henry's response, thereby expunging the personification of Peace as a woman, the Folio extends the figure. Gender and the "traffic in women," as Gayle Rubin has dubbed it, have already a figurative presence before the wooing scene proper even begins.[15] Henry, called England in this scene in the Folio, continues, "Yet leave our cousin Katharine here with us:/She is our capital demand" (V, ii, 95–96).

Henry's wooing participates in a long tradition, dating at least from the troubadours, that conflates courtship and pedagogy: it stages an erotic education. Though the king begins by asking Katherine "to teach a soldier terms/Such as will enter at a lady's ear/And plead his love-suit to her gentle heart," she is his pupil throughout. Henry speaks the same prose to the princess he uses with his captains and regulars, his social inferiors. He talks bawdily of "leapfrog," of taking "the Turk by the beard," uses colloquialisms like "jackanapes," and refers to himself proverbially as the "king of good fellows." Eleven of his eighteen speeches addressed to her end with questions to which he prompts her responses. He enumerates the tasks "Kate" might put him to for her sake, only to refuse them and substitute his own. His refusal to use the conventional language of love and his self-presentation as a plain king who knows "no way to mince it in love" are strategies of mastery, for they represent Henry as sincere, plain-spoken, a man of feeling rather than empty forms. He renames her "Kate" and finally teaches her to lay aside French manners for English customs—specifically, the kiss. The wooing scene replays the conventional female erotic plot in which a sexual encounter transforms the female protagonist and insures her destiny.[16]

In *Henry V*, Henry systematically denies Katherine's difference—her French maidenhood—and fashions her instead into an English wife. He domesticates her difference, refashioning the other as the same. When Burgundy reenters, he asks, "My royal cousin, teach you your princess English?...Is she not apt?" At the end of this second language lesson, Katherine is not only "englished" but silenced as well by the witty banter at her expense between Henry and Burgundy that excludes her from the dialogue.[17] When Henry asks the French king to "give me your daughter," he responds:

> Take her, fair son; and from her blood raise up
> Issue to me; that the contending kingdoms
> Of France and England, whose very shores look pale
> With envy of each other's happiness,
> May cease their hatred, and this dear conjunction
> Plant neighborhood and Christian-like accord
> In their sweet bosoms, that never war advance
> His bleeding sword 'twixt England and fair France.
>
> (V, ii, 366–73)

As this passage makes clear, the giving of Katherine to Henry in marriage insures relations among men, or in Lévi-Strauss's often quoted formulation: "The total relationship of exchange which constitutes marriage is not established between a man and a woman,...but between two groups of men, and the woman figures only as one of the objects in the exchange, not as one of the partners."[18] For Lévi-Strauss, the exchange of women and the male bonds it constitutes are the origin of social life. Feminists have pointed out two related consequences of Lévi-Strauss's claims. First, Julia Kristeva has debunked the seeming centrality of woman as desired object: "site of occultation or valorization, woman will be a pseudo-center, a center latent or manifest that is blatantly exposed or modestly hidden...in which man seeks man and finds him."[19] Luce Irigaray has looked not at the woman in this system of exchange but at the male bonds it insures:

> The exchanges that organize patriarchal societies take place exclusively between men,...[and if] women, signs, goods, currency, pass from man to man or risk...slipping into incestuous and endogamous relations that would paralyze all social and economic intercourse,...[then] the very possibility of the socio-cultural order would entail homosexuality. Homosexuality would be the law that regulates the socio-cultural economy.[20]

For Irigaray, the traffic in women is revealed in its coarsest aspect, deromanticized, mercantile, hyperbolic. She eroticizes the ties between men Lévi-Strauss posits to point out a continuum—which she expresses through her pun "hom(m)osexualité"—that encompasses an entire array of relations among men from the homoerotic to the competitive to the commercial. Eve Kosofsky Sedgwick has appropriated the term "homosocial" from the social sciences to describe "the whole spectrum of bonds between men, including friendship, mentorship, rivalry, institutional subordination, homosexual genitality, and economic exchange—within which the various forms of the traffic in women take place."[21]

In contemporary analyses of systems of exchange, woman's status as object is hypostasized: she is goods, chattel, substance. The category of object, and conversely that of subject—the partners in the exchange (men)—is unquestioned, despite theoretical challenges to a unified subjectivity. Feminist literary readings of exchange systems are too frequently, to parody current literary parlance, always already read. But more disturbing, such readings may reinscribe the very sex/gender system they seek to expose or change. Such a crude confrontation between subject and object betrays a naive realism: the communication between men, what Sedgwick has called homosocial relations, does not always work smoothly but is often "pathological" in ways that disrupt the traffic in women.

In his essay on the Platonic dialogue, Michel Serres explores the "pathology of communication," in which what he terms *noise* or the phenomena of interference—stammerings, mispronunciations, regional accents, as well as forms of technical interference such as background noise, jamming, static—become obstacles to communication.

He notes that Jakobson and other theoreticians of language have described dialogue as a sort of game in which the two interlocutors are united against phenomena of interference and confusion. In such a conception of dialogue, the interlocutors are in no way opposed, as in the traditional notion of dialectic, but

> are on the same side, tied together by a mutual interest: they battle together against noise. . . . *To hold a dialogue is to suppose a third man and to seek to exclude him;* a successful communication is the exclusion of the third man. The most profound dialectical problem is not the problem of the Other, who is only a variety— or a variation—of the Same, it is the problem of the third man. We might call this third man the *demon,* the prosopopoeia of noise.[22]

I want to call this third man a woman and to reconsider Serres's model of pathological communication in terms of sexual difference. *Noise,* in such a revision, the phenomena of interference, is not only dialects and mispronunciations, static and backgound noise but specificities, details, *differences.* Within a sex-gender system in which woman is the object of exchange, dialogue is homosocial, between men, and woman is the "tiers exclu" or what in a later extended meditation on this problem Serres calls "le parasite."[23] What makes Serres's model of the "tiers exclu" useful in a discussion of gender and systems of exchange is that it complicates the binary Same/Other that dominates analysis of sex/gender systems and recognizes the power of the excluded third.[24] For as Serres insists, "background noise is *essential* to communication"; the battle against the excluded third "is not always successful. In the aporetic dialogues, victory rests with the powers of noise" (67, 66).

Katherine's speech, with its mispronunciations, consistently deflects Henry's questions and solicitations. In response to his request that she teach "a soldier terms/Such as will enter at a lady's ear/And plead his love-suit to her gentle heart" (V, ii, 99–101), Katherine responds, "I cannot speak your England." When the king asks "Do you like me, Kate?" she answers "Pardonnez-moi, I cannot tell wat is 'like me.'" When he plays on her response, saying "An angel is like you, Kate, and you are like an angel," she must ask Alice "Que dit-il? que je suis semblable à les anges?" And at her "Oui, vraiment" and his "I said so, dear Katherine, and I must not blush to affirm it," she returns, "O bon Dieu! les langues des hommes sont pleines de tromperies" (115). Throughout the scene, Henry ends his speeches with questions: "What sayest thou then to my love?" and "Canst thou love me?" and Katherine responds equivocally "Is it possible dat I sould love de enemy of France?" "I cannot tell wat is dat" and "I cannot tell." Finally in response to his reiterated question "Wilt thou have me?" she responds "Dat is as it shall please de roi mon père." Assured he is so pleased, she acquiesces only to allow "Den it sall also content me." Their dialogue represents a pathological communication in which phenomena of interference both thwart the exchange and at the same time enable it. Shakespeare, unlike his analogue, The Famous Victories of Henry the Fift, represents Katherine at a linguistic disadvantage: she speaks not only French but a comically accented English and a similarly comical macaronic version of the two; but that very disadvantage becomes a strategy of equivocation and deflection.

Many readers have noted the troubling ironies generated by Henry's public justifications and private meditations, and by his military threats and disguised sojourn among his common soldiers; but his relations with Katherine, which, after all, produce the play's sense of closure, have received scant attention. Since Dr. Johnson claimed that "the poet's matter failed him in the fifth act," critics have lamented the "comic" scenes and particularly the play's ending, describing it as an "anti-climax" and Henry's wooing as "ursine."[25] Readers who bother to justify the fifth act do so with the lame defense that the ideal hero must marry and Act V is therefore the completion of Henry's character.[26] More often than not in recent "political" readings of the play, the scenes with Katherine are ignored or used to show that *Henry V* is a falling off from the earlier plays of the tetralogy. Mullaney, for example, suggests that the comic scenes exemplify Marx's "notorious" proposal "that the major events of history occur twice, once as tragedy, and again as farce"[27] and reiterates the well-worn claim that the language lesson was "borrowed" from French farce (though it certainly owes more to the popular and cheap French phrase books fashionable in socially mobile late sixteenth-century London).[28] Political readings tend to ignore the scenes altogether, thereby falling prey to the conventional assumptions of an outmoded political history that excludes social relations and gender from the domain of politics.[29]

Banishing the women's dialogue to the margins of critical discourse on *Henry V,* whether as a footnote to literary borrowing, a coda to the discussion of Falstaff and popular culture, or an absence in the "socio-political perspective of materialist criticism" is to erase gender as an historical category.[30] Gender is also the missing term in Bakhtin's enumeration of heteroglot voices.[31] Commentators have claimed that what Bakhtin terms "carnivalization" collapses hierarchic distinctions. Role reversals and the evocation of the body/bawdy are said to turn the world upside down, collapse distinctions between high culture and low, king and soldier, domination and submission. But the world turned upside down, the exchange of positions, absolute reversal, "the phase of overturning," is not enough. Reversal *preserves* the binary oppositions that ground sexual and social hierarchies: "the hierarchy of dual oppositions always reestablishes itself."[32] The disfiguring power of wordplay in the women's language lesson enables gender hierarchies, mastering the female body by dismembering it; but at the same time that very instability of linguistic meaning, the interference of noise, the o/aural dispersal of the female body, threatens linguistic mastery and successful communication not by means of reversal but through dissemination—of the body and of words.

# SEVEN

# Dressing Up: Sartorial Extravagance in Early Modern London

*M*any have broke their backs with laying manors on 'em," the Duke of Buckingham observes metaphorically in Shakespeare's *Henry VIII* (1613). In Jonson's *Epicoene* (1609) Truewit dilates his figure: "she feels not how the land drops away, nor the acres melt, nor foresees the change when the mercer has your woods for her velvets." In his *Anatomy of Melancholy* (1621) Burton forgoes metaphor but makes his point in a detailed rhetorical series: "what with shoo-ties, hangers, points, caps and feathers, scarfs, bands, cuffs, etc., in a short space...whole patrimonies are consumed." In early modern London, the relation between fashion and the failure of domestic economy was a commonplace; playwrights and poets, moralists and divines observe and criticize English prodigality in dress and its consequences, often in language as rhetorically excessive as the very fashions and spending they condemn. The relation of sartorial extravagance to the early English economy—political, linguistic, domestic—is complex. Fashion not only sank fortunes and ruined sons, it inspired and fostered new economic projects and trades for the nation; and it became an important arena in which collapsing systems of difference, social and discursive, were reconstituted in new ways.

Social historians and critics of fashion claim that in the fifteenth, sixteenth, and seventeenth centuries, extravagant dress was a class rather than a gender prerogative and adduce sumptuary legislation to support their claims.[1] Received opinion holds that since men as well as women were sartorially extravagant in the early modern period, not gender but class or status prompted both the rapidly changing patterns of dress and the frequent criticism and attempted regulation of fashion. But the argument for "class" as the hegemonic category of fashion analysis in the early modern period dismisses too easily the relation of gender to sartorial extravagance.[2] Extravagant dress was not, of course, a feature primarily of women's behavior, but it does not therefore follow that gender was not significant in the analysis of the fashion system in early modern England. In the late sixteenth century, lavish dress in men and women is increasingly described as "feminine" or "effeminate" and is part of the variety of discourses, conduct books and sermons, anatomies and travel literature, poems and plays that together produced the category "femininity" in early modern England.

DRESSING UP

The English appetite for fashionable dress was legendary by the early seventeenth century. Historians lambasted it:

> The phantisticall follie of our nation, [even from the courtier to the carter] is such, that no forme of apparell liketh us longer than the first garment is in the wearing, if it continue so long. . . .fickle headed taylors...covet to have several trickes in cutting, thereby to draw fond customers to more expense of monie.[3]

Playwrights satirized it:

> To be an accomplished gentleman, that is, a gentleman of the time, you must give over housekeeping in the country, and live altogether in the city amongst gallants; where, at your first appearance, 'twere good you *turned four or five hundred acres of your best land* into two or three trunks of apparel.[4]

Moralists lamented it:

> I am sure there is not any people under the Zodiacke of heaven, how clownish, rurall, or brutish soever, that is so poisoned with this Arsnecke of Pride, or hath drunke so deepe of the dregges of this Cup as Ailgna [England] hath; with griefe of conscience I speake it, with sorow I see it, and with teares I lament it.[5]

Foreign visitors noted it:

> They are very inconstant and desirous of novelties, changing their fashions every year, both men and women.[6]

In fact, the English preoccupation with newfangled fashion was so renowned by the mid-sixteenth century that it was represented in an emblem (fig. 9) in Andrew Boorde's *The Fyrst Boke of the Introduction of Knowledge* (1542) and widely reprinted thereafter.

In 1560, Bishop Pilkington recounted the anecdote behind Boorde's woodcut:

> I read of a painter that would paint every country man in his accustomed apparel, the Dutch, the Spaniard, the Italian, the Frenchman; but when he came to the English man, he painted

The fyrst chapter treateth of the naturall dysposicion of an Englysh man, and of the noble realme of England, & of the money that there is vsed.

I am an Englishman, and naked I stand here
Musyng in my mynde, what rayment I shal were
For now I wyll were thys and now I wyl were that
Now I wyl were I cannot tel what
All new fashyons, be plesaunt to me
I wyl haue them, whether I thryue or thee
Now I am a kryster, all men doth on me looks
What should I do, but set cocke on the hoope
what do I care, yf all the worlde me fayle
I wyll get a garment, shal reche to my tayle
Than I am a minion, for I were the new gyse

The

FIGURE NINE  Andrew Boorde, *The Fyrst Boke of the Introduction of Knowledge.* By permission of the British Library.

him naked, and gave him clothe, and bad him make it himself, for he changed his fashions so often that he knew not how to make it; such be our fickle and unstable heads, ever devising and desiring new toys.[7]

These quotations tell us a great deal about dress and fashion in early modern England. From both Harrison's *Description* and Stubbes's *Anatomy* we learn that, despite the claims of modern historians, both social and costume, concern for fashionable attire spanned the social orders from "courtier" to "carter." Harrison's vignette of the "fickle headed taylor" witnesses the growth of London as a center of conspicuous consumption, a place to see and be seen; it also attests to the development of trades that produced consumer goods and particularly a workshop economy responsive and contributing to changing fashion. The Jonson passage alludes to demographic shifts in the late sixteenth century, to social mobility and the decay of hospitality. From the Dutch traveler van Meteren we infer that the English love of sartorial novelty was not located only in the rustic's unsophisticated eye but in that of the cosmopolitan traveler as well. Van Meteren also confirms what many commentators of Elizabethan and Jacobean dress have observed: that fashion was not the province of women but the preoccupation of men and women alike. Finally, Stubbes and Pilkington's account of Boorde's woodcut witness the development of sixteenth-century overseas trade.

What did people wear that cost so much? What were the changing fashions that provoked such criticism, even astonishment? Stow's *Annales of England* is a good place to start. His account of Elizabeth's reign is punctuated by its succeeding fashions—silk hose, coaches, ruffs—and the economic changes they produced:

In the second yeere of Queene Elizabeth, one thousand five hundred and sixtie, her silke woman Mistris Mountague, presented her Maiestie, with a payre of blacke knit silke stockings, for a new yeeres gift the which after a few dayes wearing, pleased her Highnesse so weil, that shee sent for Mistris Mountague, and asked her where she had them, and if shee could helpe her to any more, who answered saying I made them very carefully of purpose only for your Maiestie, and seeing these please you so well, I will presently set more in hand, do so quoth the Queene, for indeede I like silke stockings so well because they are pleasant fine & delicate, that henceforth I will weare no more cloth stockings, and from that time unto her death, the Queene never wore any more cloath hose, but only silke stockings. . . . In the yeere 1564 Guilliam Boonen, a Dutchman, became the Queenes Coachman, and was the first that brought the use of Coaches into England.

And after a while, divers great Ladies, with as great jealousie of the Queens displeasure, made them Coaches, and rid in them up and downe the Countries, to the great admiration of all the beholders, but then by little and little they grew usuall among the Nobilitie, and others of sort, and within twentie yeeres became a great trade of Coachmaking.

In the third yeere of the Raigne of Queene Elizabeth, 1562. began the knowledge and wearing of Lawne and Cambricke, which was then brought into England by very small quantities, and when the Queene had Ruffes made thereof, for her own Princely wearing, there was none in England could tell how to starch them, for untill then all the Kinges and Queenes of England wore fine Holland in Ruffes, but the Queene made speciall meanes for some Dutch woman that could starch, and Guilliam's wife, was the first starcher the Queene had, and himselfe was the first Coachman.[8]

As the *Annales* suggest, Elizabeth's preference for silk hose, starched neckwear, and coaches spread throughout the city and the home counties. There were ruffs, of holland, linen, and cambric, sometimes edged with lace and of such prodigious size they required wire "supportasies" to make them stand; some were a third of a yard deep, as many as twelve yards full, making eating difficult and rain disastrous. Hose of worsted and silk, lined, padded with bran to turn a shapely calf and breeches of such exaggerated compass that they were outlawed. An enterprising Elizabethan accused of wearing such breeches was said to have drawn out of them "a pair of sheets, two table-clothes, ten napkins, four shirts, a brush, a glasse, a comb, and night-caps, with other things in use saying comically: 'Your lordships may understand that because I have no safer a store-house, these pockets do serve me for a room to lay my goods in.'" "Peascod-bellied" doublets were stuffed with rags to produce a broad physique and lined with damask, taffeta, or brocade slashed for display; round and wheel farthingales "bumbasted" of such scope that Stubbes claimed women wearing them seem to be "the smallest part of themselves...not women of flesh and blood, but rather puppets or mawmuts, consisting of rags and clouts compact together."[9] There were trunk-sleeves of wire, points, and laces; pomanders; hats decorated with bands, brooches, looking glasses, ribbons, favors, and feathers two feet long; garters, fringed boots, shoes with high heels of cork and adorned with elaborate shoe roses. Stow's continuer complained "men of meane rancke weare Garters, and shoe Roses, of more than five pound price," but thrifty when compared with a courtier's lined with gold and ornamented with diamond buckles at eighty pounds. Wigs were so popular that children with lovely hair were said to be accosted and shorn in the streets. In 1602 the Queen ordered payment to a certain Dorothy Speckarde for "six *heades of heare,* twelve yerdes of heare curle, one hundred devises made of heare."[10] Elizabeth was said to have eighty wigs in her wardrobe when she died; men wore "lovelocks," long, curled shocks of hair sometimes reaching to the bosom and tied with ribbons. The fashionable wore thumb rings, earrings, toothpick cases, gloves, handkerchiefs, busks, masks, bodkins, spurs useless for riding but so loud choirboys at St. Pauls's were charged with exacting "spur-money" from jingling gallants.[11]

Not only was fashion extravagant, it was big business. Silk stockings, coaches, cambric ruffs—the history of London fashion in the late sixteenth century is also the history of London commerce. By the beginning of the seventeenth century, knitted hose were standard articles of clothing. Joan Thirsk reckons "somewhere around 10 million pairs of stockings were needed to dress the whole population" and so "the domestic market could have employed about 100,000 people for 50 weeks of the year."[12] By 1599 a certain William Lee had "devised and perfected" a new technology for knitting hose and had even obtained a patent from Henry IV for his machinery.[13] Coachmaking, as the *Annales* indicate, "became a great trade" and starching a paying business.[14]

Though starch was used in the late Middle Ages, it was not produced commercially until the sixteenth-century vogue for ruffs and rebatoes. The Dutch initially supplied both the fine lawn from which ruffs were made and the starch for stiffening them, but by the 1560s starch had begun to be manufactured in England. Young London women paid twenty shillings for a Dutch woman named van der Plasse to teach them to boil starch and four or five pounds in apprenticeship fees to learn the craft entire (Thirsk, 85). By the early seventeenth century, there were said to be some nineteen starch makers in London, the same number in King's Lynn and in Norwich, "making such large quantities that every fortnight forty horseloads were taken from Norfolk to the counties of Nottinghamshire, Staffordshire, Lincolnshire, and Yorkshire." Other large producers licensed to make starch dwelt in Oxford, Northhampton, Wisbech, Ely, and Peterborough, and Thirsk claims these numbers represent only the major manufacturers (86).

Starch required so much grain in the making and had come to play so significant a part in the nation's economy by the mid-1580s that it prompted Cecil in a speech before Parliament to ask: "Is it not a very lamentable thing that we should bestow that upon starch to the setting forth of vanity and pride which would staunch the hunger of many that starve in the streets for want of bread?" (quoted in Thirsk, 88). The choice lay between a luxury tax on ruffs and curbing the starch trade. Despite his rhetorical concern for the hungry poor, Cecil chose the latter, thereby threatening the livelihood of many rather than taxing the few. The result was a royal patent and monopoly in 1588. During the famine years of the 1590s, starch-making was banned altogether and the patent revoked in the statutes against forestalling and engrossing corn (grain). Starch even provoked urban unrest: in October 1595, "a crowd forced a carman to unload a barrel of starch,"[15] but the outcry against both monopoly and prohibition finally led Elizabeth to restore "the liberty of all men" in 1601 (Thirsk, 89). Stubbes called

starch the "devil's liquor" and devotes to the wearing and preparing of ruffs a large measure of his moral ridicule. Figure 10, dated 1570, represents a starch house and offers a satiric view of the "apes" of fashion.[16]

How widespread and among what populations was the English interest and investment in fashion? I have already mentioned the evidence from Stubbes ("how clownish, rurall or brutish soever") and Harrison ("even from the courtier to the carter"). Hall recounts that Wolsey made the first serious attempt to enact sumptuary legislation and that "by his exsample many cruell officers for malice evell intreated dyverse of kynges subiectes, in so much that one Shynnynge Mayre of Rochester, set a young man on the Pillory for wering of a ryven shert."[17] Transgression of legislated dress codes was so widespread in London that the Privy Council exhorted the city to establish two watchers in each parish armed with tax roles to determine who wore what and to enforce the laws. Surveillance was also instituted for a time at the city gates, which suggests at least the perception of widespread evasion of the legislation. The statutes themselves often begin with prologues lamenting the common wearing of costly and lavish apparel. The fashion for "monstrous and outrageous greatness of hosen," for example, was said to provoke young men to "unlaweful wayes" (Hooper, 439). Jacobean city comedy is filled not only with gentlemen ruined by their sartorial tastes but with apprentices as well. In Stubbes's *Anatomy*, when Spudeus opines that ruffs and bands "are so chargeable (as I suppose) that fewe have of them," Philoponus snaps "So few have them, as almost none is without them; for every one, how meane or simple soever they bee otherwise, will have of them three or foure apeece" (Stubbes, 52). Writing in 1592, the Duke of Württemberg claimed that Englishwomen were "so dressed out in exceedingly fine clothes, and give all their attention to their ruffs and stuffs, to such a degree indeed that, as I am informed, many a one does not hesitate to wear velvet in the streets, which is common with them, whilst at home perhaps they have not a piece of dry bread" (Rye, 7–8). In *Wits Miserie* (1596), Lodge deplores "the plowman, that in times past was contented in russet, must now a daies have his doublet of the fashion, with wide cuts, his garters of fine silk Granada, to mee his Sis on Sunday. The farmer, that was contented in times past with his russet frock and mockado sleeves, now sells a cow against Easter, to buy him silken geere for his credit."[18]

In early modern England, men and women of all degrees evidently wore what they willed; Tudor sumptuary legislation attempted unsuccessfully to reinstate hierarchical social relations, increasingly jeopardized by the growing availability of fashion in the form of proliferating consumer goods. The laws were represented in ledger like fashion: in one column, clothes, styles, fabrics and accessories; in the other, the persons permitted to wear them by rank. Dress was to work as a mode of classification, a marker assigning place, age, degree, and condition; but as fashion became available to the "meaner sort," it began to lose its value as an indicator of status identity. The sumptuary statutes also served other purposes, including the protection of native English industry by prohibiting certain imports and exhorting the populace to wear the "commodities of this Realme."[19] A 1576 proclamation combines succinctly both aims: excess in apparel was said to cause "the moneyes and treasure of the Realme...[to be] yeereley conveyed out of the same, to answeare the sayde excesse; but also particulerly the wasting and undoyng of a great number of young gentlemen otherwise servisable, and others seekyng by shewe of apparel to be esteemed as gentlemen" (A-A^v). Paradoxically, sumptuary regulation may have invigorated the very excesses it sought to prohibit, as a 1559 statute reveals by proleptically prohibiting new fashions invented to evade the law. As a result of rapid technological and mercantile development, the proliferation of consumer goods, and their accessibility to a broader population, dress became an increasingly significant arena in which systems of difference were contested and reconstituted.

Dress was less a signifier of *class* or degree, as commentators on fashion and social historians have usually claimed, than a signifier of *difference* itself. In a period that witnessed the breakdown of traditional distinctions between lay and clergy, court and city, urban and rural, local and regional, literate and illiterate, to name only the most obvious, difference was problematic. The extraordinary social mobility of the late sixteenth century—generated by demographic shifts, wider access to education, a developing state bureaucracy, and the accumulation of capital through growing foreign and domestic trade—made "class" or "status" perceivable as accessible, as culturally constructed.[20] As fashion became available first to the middling sort, and then increasingly to the working classes, the differences it claimed to signify were challenged, and other means of marking difference within the fashion system were produced. The anxiety produced by these challenges to traditional, hierarchically organized systems of difference produced new modes of organizing the fashion system.

Sexual difference, as a seemingly essential, ineffaceable category became the overdetermined imaginary for organizing social distinctions. In early modern England, men dressed up, and often more elaborately than women; but increasingly when they did, they were feminized, even demonized as effeminate. At a moment when traditional categories of difference were breaking down, "femininity" represented an important, perhaps even newly essentialized, category of difference.[21] Until the 1570s, women were not treated separately in the Tudor sumptuary legislation; their mode of dress seems to have been subsumed in what was allowed their husbands or fathers. Interestingly, efforts at enforcement and recorded cases of infringement all involved men. Even the pamphlet debates and the furor over cross-dressing may owe more to an objection to women's sharing in the male privilege of *excess* in dress than to specifically masculine attire: farthingales and the voluminous breeches of the 1590s and first decade of the seventeenth century have more in common than they do differences.

Whereas moralists like Stubbes had treated male excess in dress as the foremost evil, by 1630 the London divine Martin Day aims at a different target: "they [women] are naturally inclined to the study of decking and trimming those little worldes they cary about them."[22] "Attires & ornaments are so proper to this sexe," he opines "that by most they are esteemed as the very essence of the woman, and by some againe, the purest Quintessence" (A7[r-v]). And though William Prynne in *The Unloveliness of Lovelockes* (1628) begins his attack on long hair with men, he does so by dubbing them "effeminate, degenerous, unnatural, unmanly";[23] they are "in dayly thraldome, and perpetuall bondage to their curling Irons" (A3[v]):

> Is it not now held the accomplished gallantrie of our youth, to
> Frizle their Haire like Women; and to become Womanish not
> onely in exilitie of Voyce, tendernesse of body, levitie of
> Apparell, wantonesse of Pace and Gesture, but even the very
> length, and culture of their Lockes, and Haire? (A4[r])

Prynne also displaces his anxiety by mobilizing another imagined "essential" difference for inflecting fashion—race:

> Infinite and many are the sinfull, strange, and monstrous Vanities, which this unconstant, vaine, Fantastique, Idle, Proud, Effeminate, and wanton Age of ours hath hatched, and Produced in all the parts and corners of the World; but especially in this our English climate; which like another Affricke, is alwayes bringing forth some New, some Strange, Misshapen, or Prodigious formes, and fashions, every moment. (B[r])

Prynne conflates race and the feminine in a conventional superimposition to produce Africa itself as the feminized mother giving birth to the monstrous progeny of English fashion. Clothing may, as Kaja Silverman persuasively argues following Lemoine-Luccioni, make the human body culturally visible, but in the early modern period that *cultural* visibility is inflected *essentially*.[24]

Not only was sartorial excess and its deleterious effects—ruined fortunes, monstrous births—inflected as feminine; obversely femininity became the mode of selling fashionable goods and promoting commerce. The pamphlet literature and the plays are filled with allusions to the common London practice of merchants' wives pranked up in fine clothes, sitting at the door of their shops to entice customers. Stubbes decries it, van Meteren remarks upon it, and the allusions in drama are too many to be enumerated. Tradesmen seem to have used their wives as lures, and had "seats built a purpose for such familiar entertainment" (Wilkins, 1607). In Marston's *Dutch Courtesan,* for example, a tradesman's wife is described "as proper a woman as any in Cheape. She paints now, and yet she keeps her husbands old customers to him still. In troth, a fine-fac'd wife, in a wainscot-carv'd seat, is a worthy ornament to a tradesmans shop" (III, i). Here the wife metonymically becomes the ornaments her husband sells, but in his "Satyre I" (1598) Marston is less charitable: "Gallants still resort/Unto Cornutos shop? What other cause/But chast Brownetta, Sporo thether drawes." Brownetta herself is the object Sporo and the gallants wish to purchase.

The feminization of fashion also produced, predictably enough, its trivialization, as the quotation above from Day illustrates. Words and phrases like "decking" and "trimming those little worldes" represent fashion increasingly as a woman's trivial pursuit. Prynne laments the logical obverse, the telescoping of male public responsibility—the defense of the commonwealth—to the "effeminate" practice of frizling hair: men would "rather have the Common-wealth disturbed," he complains, "then their Haire disordered" (A4[r]). Even more important than these thematized examples of the diminution of fashion is the association of fashion increasingly with goods, with the technological, the manufactured, the bought and the sold. Elizabethan and Jacobean texts are filled with attacks on fashion that enumerate endlessly the practices and details of dress, from recipes for cosmetics to whiten the face and hands to the satirists' lists of fashion details that are always relegated either to descriptions of the female characters or the feminized gallant or fop.

Feminist critics have pointed out the persistent association, particularly in aesthetics, between the decorative and the feminine. Naomi Schor begins *Reading in Detail* with the question, "Is the detail feminine?" and goes on to outline the way in which the history of aesthetic theory devalues the decorative. She quotes Gombrich, who observes the "identification of crowded ornament with feminine taste" and traces that identification historically back to the rhetorical manuals of classical antiquity and forward to modern treatises on taste.[25] The ornamental, she points out, is associated with "anarchic proliferation" said to produce anxiety and restlessness. In early modern England, newly proliferating consumer goods and the anxiety, even alienation, that capital produced was displaced onto the feminine and the non-elite and symptomatically represented in the frequently deployed grammatical series that enumerating the details of fashionable English dress.

But cultural constructions are never seamless, and the anxieties generated by the massive social and political changes of the early modern period and displaced onto the feminine were never fully contained. Just as "class" had become culturally visible in the books and schools of conduct and courtiership, something to achieve rather than something natural or given, so sexual difference came to be represented as itself a constructed category, as what we call "gender." City comedy is filled with "recipes" for femininity, descriptions of female "piec'd beauty" that could be bought in the exchanges and shops along the Strand. Femininity became an available imaginary, a simulated womanhood represented strikingly in descriptions of the female toilette.[26] When the "woman" being dressed is a boy, femininity is foregrounded as masquerade or "hyperfemininity," as in the following passage from *Lingua* (1607)

> Five hours ago I set a dozen maids to attire a boy like a nice
> gentlewoman; but there is such doing with their looking-glasses,
> pinning, unpinning, setting, unsetting, formings and
> conformings; painting blue veins and cheeks; such stir with
> sticks and combs, cascanets, dressings, purls, falls, quares, busks,

bodies, scarfs, necklaces, carcanets, rebatoes, borders, tires, fans, palisodoes, puffs, ruffs, cuffs, muffs, pusles, fusles, parlets, frislets, bandlets, fillets, crosslets, pendulets, amultes, that yet she's scarce dressed to the girdle; and now there is such calling for fardingales, kirtles, busk-points, shoe-ties, &c., that seven pedlars' shops—nay, all Stourbridge fair, will scarce furnish her. A ship is sooner rigged by far, than a gentlewoman made ready.[27]

Here the "anarchic proliferation" of the necessaries of fashion trans- forms the boy into a gentlewoman even though he is never finally "made ready." Though the passage begins with a simile, the boy will be attired "like a gentlewoman," the force of the series enumerating the practices and commodities of femininity turns him into the "she" of line 9. The first series, with its antitheses ("pinning, unpinning, set- ting, unsetting"), emphasizes the process of dressing and the produc- tion of the feminine "she." Painting serves not merely to heighten the "natural" color of cheek and lip; it produces the "natural" body through the limning of veins. The playful neologisms of the final and absurdly long series elaborate the details of fashionable dress extrava- gantly, a forceful demonstration of the link between the feminine de- tail and a growing consumer economy. These items of a gentlewoman's toilet ironically are sold by humble peddlers and at public fairs.

At IV, iv, of *Every Man Out of His Humour,* the fop Fastidious Brisk describes the articles of his fashionable dress injured in a duel. They include his "wrought" shirt: men's and women's linen, worn secreted beneath their outer clothing, was often embroidered by women with representations not only of decorative fruits and flowers but with texts, passages of history, poetry and scripture, an appropriation of "femi- nine" accomplishments in the service of writing. But rhetorical and sartorial styles were intertwined not only in the intricately worked shirts beneath a gentleman's doublet; language that transgressed the ideals of decorum and fitness was troped as fashion and inveighed against in similar terms. In a famous passage from *Discoveries* (1641), Jonson draws the analogy explicitly: "Wheresoever, manners, and fash- ions are corrupted, Language is. It imitates the publicke riot. The excesses of Feasts, and apparrell, are the notes of a sick State; and the wantonnesse of language, of a sick mind."[28] Excess, of food or fashion, means corruption—moral, linguistic, national. A striking example from Dekker illustrates: "An English-mans suite is like a traitors bodie that hath beene hanged, drawne, and quartered, and is set up in several places: his Codpiece is in Denmarke, the coller of his Dublet and the belly in France; the wing and narrow sleeve in Italy; the short waste hangs over a Dutch Botchers stall in Utrich; his huge sloppes speakes spanish; Polonia gives him the Bootes" (Zwager, 110). Here the mingle-mangle of English fashion is displaced onto national "others" and xenophobia worked out through a spectacular and psychically useful synecdochic substitution of the traitor's body for the nation-state. The Elizabethans sought to police rhetorical styles as vigorously as they tried to police fashion.

For Jonson, the excess of apparel is to the state what wantonness of language is to the sick mind; tropes from the world of fashion were used to figure the improper use of language and the moral failure both represent. Later Jonson spins out the analogy:

> But now nothing is good that is naturall: Right and naturall language seeme to have least of the wit in it; that which is writh'd and tortur'd, is counted the more exquisite. Cloath of Bodkin, or Tissue, must be imbrodered; as if no face were faire, that were not pouldred, or painted? No beauty to be had, but in wresting, and writhing our owne tongue? Nothing is fashionable, till it be deform'd; and this is to write like a *Gentleman*. All must bee as affected, and preposterous as our Gallants claothes, sweet bags, and night-dressings: in which you would thinke our men lay in; like *Ladies:* it is so curious. (26)

Here Jonson advocates a plain style that he equates with plain clothes; he deplores the ornate, which he terms "writh'd and tortur'd." The linguistic worlds of dress, cosmetics, the body, and strangely, torture and punishment, are collapsed. Clothes already pierced with a bodkin—the instrument used to make holes for the "points" (the lacings of flamboyant Elizabethan and Jacobean sleeves)—and tissue (fabric woven with gold and silver thread) must be further embellished with embroidery to be fashionable. A face must be powdered or painted to be fair, but the "as if" clause, a conditional clause of comparison, works its comparison both ways, collapsing clothes and the body. "Writhe" illustrates this collapse of categories: the verb meant to twist, bend, coil, or fold, particularly into a wreath, and specifically to plait. Plaiting and pleating, along with embroidery, was specifically prohibited those beneath the status of knight in the 1559 sumptuary statutes, that is, sumptuary legislation regulated not only fabrics—velvet, silk, furs, cloth of gold and silver—but styles of dress as well. The verb also meant to contort the body and limbs from emotion or stimulation and finally (as did "wrest") to pervert the meaning of a text, passage, or word. To write "like a gentlemen" is to write a deformed prose, as preposterous as the fashionable clothes worn by city gallants; but those fashions are explicitly feminized: pomanders, and particularly night gowns "in which you would thinke our men lay in; like Ladies: it is so curious." Jonson betrays his sexual anxiety in his use of the conditional in the fantastic image of men in feminine deshabille.

In a later passage, Jonson continues and develops these figures with a marginal gloss "de mollibus & effaeminatis":

> *There* is nothing valiant, or solid to bee hop'd for from such, as are alwayes kempt'd, and perfum'd; and every day smell of the Taylor. The exceedingly curious, that are wholly in mending such an imperfection in the face, in taking away the Morphew in the neck; or bleaching their hands at Mid-night, gumming, and bridling their beards, or making the waste small, binding it with hoopes, while the mind runs at waste: Too much pickednesse is not manly. Not from those that will jeast at their owne outward imperfections, but hide their ulcers within, their Pride, Lust, Envie, ill nature, with all the art and authority they can. These persons are in danger. (56)

At stake in Jonson's comparisons is not only the notion that language is merely the dress of thought—the now conventional binaries of inner and outer, with the inward valued as virtuous and manly, the outward deplored as superficial and feminine—but also a view of subjectivity we have come to call the bourgeois subject.

But Jonson's defense of the natural, the inward, the manly, is car-

ried out in anything but the plain style; his own is as elaborately figured and periodically complex, as characterized by exaggeration and
by the detailed series, as the "effeminate" language he berates.
Jonson's hegemonic rhetoric is everywhere "haunted by what it excludes, subverted by what it subordinates,"[29] by a femininity that, however proscribed, provides a pleasure he cannot forego.

# City Talk:
# Femininity and
# Commodification
# in Jonson's
# Epicoene

*In the liveliest London streets, the shops press one against the other, shops which flaunt behind their hollow eyes of glass all the riches of the world, Indian cashmeres, American revolvers, Chinese porcelains, French corsets, Russian furs and tropical spices; but all these things promising the pleasures of the world bear those deadly white labels on their fronts on which are engraved arabic numerals with laconic characters—£, s, d (pound sterling, shilling, pence). This is the image of commodities as they appear in circulation.*

Marx, *A Contribution to the Critique of Political Economy*[1]

Against his great house in the Strand, the enterprising Earl of Salisbury opened "Britain's Burse" in 1609; within the year, Jonson's *Epicoene* was first produced. With its galleries and arcades lined with shops licensed to carry luxury goods, and its upper rooms available for meeting and conversation, the New Exchange, as it came to be called, was immediately a place of both erotic and economic exchange. Already in 1619, a contemporary observer remarked that "thy shops with prettie wenches swarm,/Which for thy custome are a kind of charme/To idle gallants."[2] There and in the nascent West End, as Stow's great Survey of London reminds us,

> Their shops made a very gay Shew, by the various foreign Commodities they were furnished with; and, by the Purchasing of them, the People of *London,* and of other Parts of *England,* began to spend extravagantly; whereof great Complaints were made among the graver Sort. There were but a few of these Milliners Shops in the Reign of King *Edward the Sixth,* not above a Dozen in all *London;* but, within forty Years after, about the Year 1580, from the City of *Westminster* along to *London,* every Street became full of them. Some of the Wares sold by these Shop-keepers were, Gloves made in *France* or *Spain,* Kersies of *Flanders* Dye, *French* cloth or Frizado, Owches, Brooches, Agglets made in *Venice* or *Milan,* Daggers, Swords, Knives, Girdles of the *Spanish* Make, Spurs made at *Milan, French* or *Milan* caps, Glasses, painted Cruses, Dials, Tables, Cards, Balls, Puppets, Penners, Inkhorns, Toothpicks, Silk-Bottoms and Silver-Bottoms, fine earthen Pots, Pins and Points, Hawks-Bells, Saltcellars, Spoons, Dishes of Tin. Which made such a Shew in the Passengers Eyes, that they could not but gaze on them, and buy some of these knicknacks, though to no Purpose necessary.[3]

Stow's sketch of mercantile London in the early seventeenth century bears an uncanny resemblance to Marx's description of the British metropolis almost two hundred fifty years later. Immediately striking is the sheer proliferation of goods, their variety in kind and provenance, and their mode of presentation as spectacle. Commodities offer the buyer access to a larger world, from the far-flung cities of Europe that were early modern England's access to the east, to the

American cowboys and Russian winters of Marx's sketch of nine-teenth-century London. Both suggest prodigious excess and the de-mise of the rare—in short, commodification. And for both, the se-ries—the list of substantives with their respective qualifiers, cosmopolitan or colonial—offers the reader-cum-buyer the consumer pleasures Stow and Marx describe.

But there are also, of course, striking differences. Whereas the Stow account bears witness to England's expanding maritime power after 1588 and to growing mercantile relations with Europe, Marx's list of goods testifies to Britain's imperial conquests and world power in the mid-nineteenth century and alludes at least to mass production and the development of manufacturing. The *Survey* is characteristi-cally conservative in its solidarity with the "graver Sort" and its critique of London's growth as a center of "conspicuous consumption" where shoppers buy "knicknacks, though to no purpose necessary." The enu-meration of Stow's series tends to trivialize the goods named, whereas Marx aggrandizes what he describes—they are "all the pleasures of the world"—but his cosmic tribute is deflated by his ironic periphrasis on "deadly" price tickets that reduce variety to identity: from Russia to America to the Orient, these goods are all for sale. Consumption in Marx is revealed to be a function of production rather than access to cosmic expanse and pleasure. Abundance and desire are revealed as scarcity and lack.[4]

Work in political economy has sometimes idealized preindustrial cultures, posing them as versions of an economic pastoral, golden ages of household production and self-sufficiency before commodification. Recently that nostalgic cliché has been challenged as scholars have begun to study the changing world of goods in early modern Europe: not only the quantity and ownership of objects but their character, how they were acquired and displayed—objects as representations of a culture and its codes, and ownership not merely as a material fact but fashioned by conventions. Historians have recognized increasingly the role taste and cultural innovation have played in the development of international trade and patterns of economic growth. Such changes in the early modern material environment were both produced by and had enormous impact on social relations.[5]

Women's relation to the processes of commodification has been situated in a variety of ways. Targeted in the modern period as the primary consumers of proliferating goods, and frequently addressed by advertisers seeking to create markets, women have been represented not only as consumers but as goods themselves, and inversely, goods have often been feminized. Baudrillard writes of what he terms the feminization of objects, the object-as-woman as the privileged myth of consumer persuasion: "Tous les objets se font femmes pour être achetés."[6] Marx often conceptualized commodity exchange in terms of the object-as-woman in *Capital,* where he uses imagery first of seduction, then rape, to define commodity relations: "Commodities cannot themselves go to market and perform exchanges in their own right. We must, therefore, have recourse to their guardians, who are the possessors of commodities. Commodities are things, and therefore lack the power to resist man. If they are unwilling, he can use force; in other words, he can take possession of them." Marx glosses this analysis of commodities with a note that reveals the intersection of commodification, women and, interestingly, literary representation: "In the twelfth century, so renowned for its piety, very delicate things often appear among these commodities. Thus a French poet of the period enumerates among the commodities to be found in the fair at Lendit, alongside clothing, shoes, leather, implements of cultivation, skins, etc., also *femmes folles de leurs corps.*"[7] In equating women and things, Marx betrays a certain anxiety, evinced in his choice of a poetic authority, his euphemism for describing prostitutes, and his lapse into French. Women's relation to commodities is multiple, even extravagant: at once goods, sellers of goods, and consumers of goods. Significantly, in Marx's formulation, the object-as-woman is defined in terms of lack: goods "lack the power to resist man."

The proliferation of goods described in the *Survey* and their availability for sale in the London exchanges and the growing West End represent an early episode in the process of commodification under capitalism. Goods from the continent and from more exotic lands were for the first time available in numbers in England: tobacco, porcelain, imported textiles, metalwork.[8] In the early seventeenth century woman became the target of contemporary ambivalence toward that process. She is represented in the discourses of Jacobean London as at once consumer and consumed: her supposed desire for goods is linked to her sexual availability.

Marriage sermons, conduct books, popular forms such as plays, ballads, and jest books—in short, the discourses that managed and produced femininity in the late sixteenth and early seventeenth centuries—all conflate the sexual and the economic when representing feminine desire. Bullinger's popular handbook, *The Christian State of Matrimony,* translated in England by Myles Coverdale, includes a lively dramatic dialogue also quoted in chapter 2, in which the whore ridicules her client, "No more money, no more love."[9] Thomas Becon complained that women were moved to every kind of sexual dishonesty for as little as a "morsel of bread or a potte of bear."[10] Though examples of this conflation could be considerably multiplied, more important for my purpose is the synecdochic representation of feminine desire—sexual or acquisitive—as an open mouth.[11] The whore's insatiable genitals were represented as a thirsty mouth, and the talking woman was everywhere equated with a voracious sexuality that in turn abetted her avid consumerism: scolds were regularly accused of both extravagance and adultery.

Talk in women then is dangerous because it is perceived as a usurpation of multiple forms of authority, a threat to order and male sovereignty, to masculine control of commodity exchange, to a desired hegemonic male sexuality. The extent of this perceived threat may be gauged by the strict delegation of the talking woman to the carefully defined and delimited spheres of private and domestic life in which the husband was exhorted to rule. In the Renaissance, as many commentators have pointed out, even those humanists most progressive in their advocacy of women's worth insisted vehemently that rhetoric and public speaking were anathema to women.[12] Whenever women's talk removed to public spaces, it became a threat; when it burst out of the house and into the streets or village, town or city, or when it took place in the church or alehouse, it became dangerous, even seditious. Traditionally excluded from public life, from government affairs, law courts, and the pulpit, women enter the public sphere of early seventeenth-century London by going to market, both to buy and to sell.[13]

Jonson's *Epicoene* is peopled with talkative women whom he portrays as monstrous precisely because they gallivant about the city streets spending breath as well as money.[14] His talking women are not merely the butts of satire but are represented as monstrously unnatural because they threaten masculine authority. Not domestic gossips who meet at home, Jonson's women are

> ladies that call themselves the Collegiates, an order between courtiers and country-madams, that live from their husbands and give entertainment to all the Wits and Braveries o' the time, as they call 'em, cry down or up what they like or dislike in a brain or a fashion with most masculine or rather hermaphroditical authority, and every day gain to their college some new probationer. (I, i, 68–74)[15]

Their college apes contemporary educational institutions and associations for men, and they perform the activities of their "foundation" before an audience, the Wits and Braveries; significantly, it is the voicing of their critical opinions abroad ("down and up") that makes them monstrous.[16]

In the main plot when the silent woman begins at last to speak, Morose wails "O immodesty! A manifest woman" (III, iv, 37). Speech makes her sex immediately, if ironically, apparent to Morose and witnesses her usurpation of masculine authority within the family, that seventeenth-century "little commonwealth": "I'll have none of this co-acted, unnatural dumbness in my house, in a family where I govern" (47–49), she explains, to which Morose responds "She is my regent already! I have married a Penthesilea, A Semiramis, sold my liberty to a distaff" (50–51). Morose figures the talking woman as Amazonian, as a warrior queen, and Epicoene bears out his fears in the next scene when she commands that the door be left open to her friends and promises to "see him that dares move his eyes toward it" (III, v, 31). Morose also immediately assumes that her speech indicates sexual transgression: "I have married his [Cutbeard's] cittern, that's common to all men" (54–55).

Morose's fear of noise, which is presented as generalized at the outset of the play, becomes increasingly gender specific. In Act I we learn that he hates hawking fishwives and orange women, chimney sweeps and broom men, metal workers, braziers, armorers, pewterers, and the "waits" or wind instrumentalists maintained at public expense to play on holidays or other special occasions in the city streets. His house lies on a street "so narrow at both ends that it will receive no coaches" (I, i, 150–51), a status symbol Epicoene promises to buy instantly on her marriage. The "perpetuity of ringing"—the bells that marked the hours and tasks of daily life and also knelled deaths in plague time—drive him to a padded cell: "a room with double walls and treble ceilings, the windows close shut and calked" (I, ii, 166–68). But as the plot unfolds, Morose's early universal fear of noise is identified increasingly with women. Though the gallants are noisy, woman becomes the overdetermined locus of noise, the screen on which Morose's agoraphobia is projected: "He has employed a fellow this half year all over England to harken him out a dumb woman. Her silence is dowery enough" (21–23). The city woman tropes urban vices: the noise, the crowd, sexuality, and consumerism. Even her oneiric life is bound up with the city: Mrs. Otter, when she recounts her dream to Clerimont, says "anything I do but dream o' the city" (III, ii, 57).

Jonson presents in luxuriant detail the attractions of London for ladies. In Truewit's attempt to dissuade Morose from marriage, he details the pastimes of city women's lives, their infinite consuming desires: "she must have that rich gown for such a great day, a new one for the next, a richer for the third; be served in silver; have the chamber filled with a succession of grooms, footmen, ushers and other messengers, besides embroiderers, jewelers, tire-women, sempsters, feathermen, perfumers" (II, ii, 87–92). She comes to the city seeking to "be a stateswoman" (95–96), a satiric coinage, as the Yale editor notes. Truewit's modern city woman enjoys public affairs, must "know all the news," and evidently reads widely "so she may censure poets and authors and styles and compare 'em, Daniel with Spenser, Jonson with t'other youth" (97–99). The ladies complain that Morose's "nuptials want all marks of solemnity....No gloves? No garters? No scarves? No epithalamium? No masque?" (III, vi, 74–75, 80). These women are consummate consumers, of poems and plays in the same breath as gloves and garters. They frequent the court, tiltings, public shows and feasts, playhouses, even church to show off their clothes, "to see and to be seen" (VI, i, 54).

Favorite haunts of the collegiates are the Strand which teemed with shops, the china houses, and the New Exchange, a Renaissance shopping mall. Truewit admonishes Morose against marriage by inveighing against woman as consumer in a conventional metaphor often repeated in the early seventeenth century: "She feels not how the land drops away, nor the acres melt, nor forsees the change when the mercer has your woods for her velvets" (II, ii, 92–94). Men and the traditional landed values of the elite are pitted against a burgeoning consumer culture Jonson and his contemporaries identify as feminine. In 1632, Donald Lupton complained of the exchanges:

> Here are usually more Coaches attendent, then at Church doores: The Merchants should keep their wives from visiting the Upper Roomes too often, least they tire their purses, by attyring themselves....There's many Gentle-women come hither, that to help their faces and Complexions, breakes their husbands backs, who play foule in the Country with Their Land, to be faire; and play false in the City.[17]

Epicoene promises to join the ladies in their shopping sprees and promenades "three or four days hence...when I have got me a coach and horses" (IV, vi, 15–16), a powerful emblem of late sixteenth- and early seventeenth-century urban life and status. Consumption is presented as a feminine preoccupation and pastime in the discourses of Jacobean England, indulged in by women and feminized men like the fop Amorous La Foole, the object of similar satire. Women are both consumers and commodities: Otter slanders his wife by exclaiming in a parodic *blason* that her "teeth were made i' the Blackfriars, both her eyebrows i' the Strand, and her hair in Silver Street. Every part o' the town owns a piece of her" (IV, II, 88–90). Women's "pieced beauty" (I, i, 77) is demystified, revealed as goods that are bought and sold in the shopping streets of the city.[18]

In *Epicoene,* the talking woman represents the city *and* what in large part motivated the growth of the city: mercantilism and colonial expansion. Consumption, like female talk, is presented as at once stereotypical (women all do it) and as unnatural (women who do it are masculine, hermaphroditical, monstrous). Critics of *Epicoene* typically discuss its female characters in terms of the opposition between the hermaphroditical, monstrous epicene women and the cultural norm—women who were chaste, silent, and obedient. The play's satire depends on shared, if unrepresented, assumptions about behavior appropriate to women that position the audience to perceive the collegiates' activities as reprehensible. Such readings join Jonson in his censure by assuming the implicit norm as positive and "natural" rather than culturally produced. In Jonson, woman is the focus of cultural ambivalence toward social mobility, urbanization, and colonialism; she is the site of systems of exchange that constituted capitalism, the absolutist state, and English colonial power. Mrs. Otter, after all, owes to the China trade the fortune that enables her both to rule Captain Otter as his "Princess" (III, i) and to aspire to a more prestigious class position.[19]

*Epicoene* dramatizes the discursive slippage between women's talk, women's wealth, and a perceived threat to male authority. But this intersection of woman, the city, and consumerism was not only a literary phenomenon; contemporary observers of early Stuart London from the king himself to men like John Chamberlain witness it as well. Whereas Elizabeth issued proclamations and statutes against building, dividing houses, and an excess of apprentices, in order to curb the growth of London, James directed his anxiety about the growth of London against women as consumers.[20] In June 1608, perhaps six months to a year before *Epicoene* was first performed, the king railed at "those swarms of gentry who, through the instigation of their wives and to new model and fashion their daughters (who, if they were unmarried, marred their reputations, and if married, lost them) did neglect their country hospitality, and cumber the city, a general nuisance to the kingdom."[21] The pursuit of London fashion in James's formulation leads not only to overpopulation but apparently to sexual transgression, since gentry daughters lose their reputations in their eager migration to the metropolis. The king often reiterated such proclamations: in a major speech before the Star Chamber in 1616, James opined that "one of the greatest causes of all gentlemens desire, that haue no calling or errand, to dwell in London, is apparently the pride of women. For if they be wiues, then their husbands; and if they be maydes, then their fathers must bring them up to London because the new fashion is to bee had no where but in London."[22] John Chamberlain reports that "even upon Christmas eve came foorth another proclamation, for their wives and families and widowes to be gon like-wise, and that hence-forward gentlemen should remain here during termes only or other busines, without bringing their wives and fami-lies, which is *durus sermo* to the women."[23] In Jacobean London, women were held accountable for urban ills.

Not only are historical and cultural formations important to read-ing *Epicoene;* so are the linguistic economies Jonson deploys to repre-sent the relation of women and consumption, that is, his *means* of representing women and goods. Jonson's comedies might be charac-terized generally by a fondness for *copia* enacted through the gram-matical series. In the reverse *blason* quoted earlier, or Truewit's enu-meration of the evils of marriage, Jonson betrays a penchant for the list. In his study of Shaw's style, Richard Ohmann analyzes Shavian modes of order, particularly in the series. In a series, Ohmann shows, equivalences are set up that typically end with a summation, an "in short" or other phrase that subsumes and extends what precedes it. Even without such summative devices, the grammatical construction of a series implies a relationship of equivalence, and particularly "when the series ends with 'and so forth' 'and the like,' or 'etc.'" Such phrases invite the reader to continue, "to extrapolate the class in the direction pointed by the given portion of the extension. [The reader] must have grasped the rubric under which members are alike." The Shavian series, Ohmann claims, typically "does not exhaust the class it defines" but stops short, demanding "that the reader infer similar-ity."[24] Though Ohmann's concern is similarity, more important to my argument is the productive power of the series, its demand on the reader or audience. The series, seemingly excessive and extravagant, paradoxically produces lack or scarcity and the desire for more.

In *Epicoene* the series is most often used to describe women, to set up invidious equivalences that stop short but position the audience to produce more. After marriage is defined by a long series detailing increasingly perverse ways of committing suicide, Jonson sums them up with "any way rather than to follow this goblin Matrimony" (II, ii, 27). After marrying, Truewit threatens, a man's wife may run away "with a vaulter, or the Frenchman that walks upon ropes, or him that dances the jig, or a fencer for his skill at his weapon" (50–52), a short series that does a great deal of cultural work with its bawdy innuendo

and its class prejudice. Women's behavior as consumers is then represented in the torrential series quoted above, which equates female
consumption and sexual misconduct. It ends with Truewit's summative "one thing more, which I had almost forgot" in which Jonson links
sexual transgression and economic power: the woman "whom you are
to marry, may have made a conveyance of her virginity aforehand, as
your wise widows do of their states, before they marry, in trust to some
friend" (119–20). Typically in *Epicoene,* the Jonsonian series enumerates a list of female activities or behaviors but stops short leaving the
audience not with a feeling of completion or abundance, but of lack.

In Jonson's series, or the list of goods from Stow's *Survey* with
which I began, the series suggests abundance, profusion, availability.
But as Marx's description reminds us, the proliferation of goods and
serial multiplicity systematically produce want, a dialectic of scarcity.
Commodity pleasures—the more you have, the more you want. On a
psychoanalytic axis, consumption figures not possession but lack, the
woman's part. The series seems to democratize things: separated only
by commas or the semi-colon, the items of a series hurtle along pell-
mell seemingly without distinctions, enacting a sort of grammatical
commodification; but instead of erasing differences, the grammatical
series, like commodification itself, systematizes privilege and difference. In Jonson, sexual difference is the axis along which commodification is plotted, with privilege or class as a destabilizing vari-
ant: the aspiring Mrs. Otter is of a decidedly lower status than the
collegiates, but the relation of all the women to commodification is
represented as alike, which tends to level class differences. In Marx,
class is the constant, but sexual difference is the variable that problematizes his class analysis of commodification.

I would like to end with an episode in what I would term cultural
politics rather than cultural poetics: a look at the earliest stage history
of *Epicoene,* which takes me back as well to the establishment of the
New Exchange with which I began. The historian Thomas Wilson,
Salisbury's agent, tells the story, recorded in the *State Papers Domestic,*
that the Earl had first proposed to call his new mercantile enterprise[25]
"Armabell" as a compliment to a lady. That lady is said to have been
Arbella Stuart, whose complaint about a supposed allusion to her person led to the play's suppression after its first or an early performance.

Daughter of James's uncle Charles Stewart, great granddaughter of Henry VIII's sister Margaret Tudor, related as well to Bess of Hardwick, learned lady and dedicatee of Aemilia Lanier—Arbella Stuart was next in line to the English throne after James and believed by some, because of her English upbringing, better qualified than he. Had she been, in Portia's words, "accomplished/With that we lack," she might well have succeeded. Elizabeth kept her under house arrest for years fearing her marriage and plots against the throne. James's first diplomatic instructions to the Scottish ambassador in London after his mother's execution were to secure a declaration from Elizabeth that James was the rightful heir and to engage "that the Lady Arbella be not given in marriage without the King's special advice and consent."[26] The Venetian ambassador Nicolo Molin sent the following account of Arbella Stuart to his government in 1607:

> The nearest relative the King has is Madame Arabella, descended from Margaret, daughter of Henry VII, which makes her cousin to the King. She is twenty-eight; not very beautiful, but highly accomplished, for besides being of most refined manners she speaks fluently Latin, Italian, French, Spanish, reads Greek and Hebrew, and is always studying. She is not very rich, for the late Queen was jealous of everyone, and especially of those who had a claim on the throne, and so she took from her the larger part of her income, and the poor lady cannot live as magnificently nor reward her attendants as liberally as she would. The King professes to love her and hold her in high esteem. She is allowed to come to Court, and the King promised when he ascended the throne, that he would restore her property, but he has not done so yet, saying that she shall have it all and more on her marriage, but so far the husband has not been found, and she remains without mate and without estate.[27]

Deprived of her ancestral estates and income, Arbella Stuart nevertheless spent lavishly in accordance with her position at court and was continually in debt; Chamberlain describes her as rivaling the queen in dress and jewels.[28] In the months preceding the production of *Epicoene*, Arbella Stuart was the subject of rumor at court. Called to account before the council, she disputed claims that she had been converted to Catholicism or planned to marry without the king's consent. She complained forcefully of the failed restoration of her patrimony and of her poverty, and succeeded in winning some relief from James. But throughout this period she was surreptitiously engaged in a courtship that issued in her clandestine marriage to William Seymour in 1611. When the king learned of their marriage, Arbella Stuart was again arrested and given into the custody of the Bishop of York. In a daring escape reminiscent of the plots of countless Renaissance comedies and romances, Arbella herself played an epicene part. Disguised as a boy, she managed to elude her jailor and fled, chased by the king's authorities, across the channel to meet her husband of seventeen days in Ostend where she was finally apprehended. The solicitor general who presided at the subsequent trial figured her transgression as childish disobedience, chiding her for "transacting the most weighty and binding part and action of her life, which is marriage, without acquainting his Majesty, which had been a neglect even to a mean parent."[29] Imprisoned in the Tower, she died in 1615. According to modern commentators, she died insane, but contemporaries were more skeptical of the reports that she was mad. In 1613, Chamberlain wrote twice to friends that the "Lady Arbella is saide to be distracted which (yf yt be so) comes well to passe for somebody whom they say she hath neerly touched."[30] Chamberlain realized the threat she posed to the king.

The relation of Arbella Stuart to Jonson's *Epicoene* is more than an episode in stage history. The play attacks "hermaphroditical" talking women, women who transgress the culturally constructed codes of behavior believed appropriate to them in early modern England. Arbella Stuart, "a regular termagant,"[31] often refused to stay at court, preferring to live independently and often writing to friends of her wish for time with her books. Contemporaries always mention her propensity for study and claimed it made her melancholic, a common result, according to Renaissance humors theory, of too much study and learning. The melancholic, of course, was said to favor solitude and to be prone to distraction. The frequently repeated claims that Arbella Stuart died mad figures her political transgression in private terms, within the medical discourse of female hysteria. The judgment "died insane" safely categorizes women who transgress their culture's sex/gender codes by studying, marrying without their "parent's" consent, spending extravagantly, in bed or in shops. Arbella Stuart suffered for transgressing cultural norms, and for a brief moment, she made Jonson's *Epicoene* suffer with her.

The discourses around Arbella Stuart in *State Papers, Foreign and Domestic* are remarkably consistent with the major themes and preoccupations of Jacobean city comedy and particularly *Epicoene:* the topoi of the shrew and the learned lady, the problems of marriage and inheritance, the political aspirations of women, the position of women as consumers. But as with the comparison of Marx and Stow with which I began, there are also important differences. Arbella Stuart's marriage, her spending and debt, are part of an aristocratic ethos of status and degree foreign to the aspirations of Stuart London's "middling sort." To ally the story of Arbella Stuart to city comedy occludes the status-differentiated histories of seventeenth-century women even as it recognizes a shared position in the Jacobean sex/gender system.

But the telling of Arbella Stuart's story cannot stand unremarked at the end of my argument: the historical anecdote has become notorious, impugned by opposing camps in literary studies. Insofar as it has been used to ground literary interpretation in the so-called "facts" of history, the critique of the new historicist anecdote is justified; but insofar as that critique, mounted either by the literary critic deferential to an imagined scienticity of history, or by the historian claiming for history an archival high ground of "Truth," that critique represents a refusal of the challenges posed by theories of reading and poststructuralism. Stories are fields of struggle, as Lynn Hunt has phrased it,[32] hermeneutic arenas in which we contend not for a material ground that is not language, but for meaning and its effects. How we read Arbella Stuart's story determines a whole series of categories and critical questions: how we understand elite and bourgeois women's lives and the management of femininity in early modern England; how we understand Elizabethan and Jacobean political history; how we analyze the relation of playwright to contemporary culture; and how we conceive and represent female subjectivity.

# EPILOGUE

*I* n *Reading Capital,* Althusser theorizes a practice of reading by
analyzing Marx's commentary on nineteenth-century political
economy. In what Althusser calls a *first reading,* Marx reads his predecessors, Smith and Ricardo, and sees what they miss: labor. His reading, then, is based on seeing what they overlooked, on *oversights* or
*bévues.* Althusser points out that this stage of reading remains fixed in
a specular economy. Locked in "the mirror myth of knowledge," this
stage of reading depends on vision, on sight and oversight, presences
and absences, and always assumes the possibility of seeing clearly.[1]

But Althusser goes on to demonstrate that in Marx's reading of
political economy there is a *"second quite different reading"* not based on
mirroring or limited to "objects that can be seen so long as one's eyes
are clear":

> What political economy does not see is not a pre-existing object
> which it could have seen but did not see—but an object which it
> produced itself in its operation of knowledge....Through the la-
> cunary terms of its new answer political economy produced a
> new question, but "unwittingly." It made "a complete change in
> the terms of the 'original' problem," and thereby produced a
> new problem, but without knowing it....It remained convinced
> that it was still on the terrain of the old problem, whereas it has
> "unwittingly changed terrain."[2]

Readings of Renaissance plays and revisions of the canon that "see"
the woman who has been overlooked leave intact a reading practice
that depends on seeing more clearly than before, through a long
genealogy of readers, each seeing what his predecessor overlooked.
Such a practice of reading leaves unexamined the quality of literari-
ness as well as its related hermeneutic practice of literary interpretation.

In my reading of now-canonical Renaissance plays, I have willfully shifted my focus away from the exclusively literary, and tried to gesture toward, in Althusser's terms, the production of a different theoretical *problematic*. On such a terrain of reading, it is not simply a question of *seeing* the woman, of putting "woman" into discursive circulation, but of changing the terms of reading by mobilizing a variety of texts and stories—theoretical, canonical, archival, historical, from Marx and Stow, Derrida, Foucault and Baudrillard, Shakespeare and Jonson, Elizabeth and James, the Venetian ambassadors, Agnes Waterhouse, to name only a few. We need a different kind of textual intercourse, a promiscuous conversation of many texts, early modern elite and non-elite, historical records and ideological discourses, contemporary theory and popular culture, that puts into play the "literary," the "historical," "gender," as relations and positions rather than static categories, a practice already at work in the United States in examples of the "new historicism," in Britain under the rubric "cultural materialism," and in feminist theory. Such intercourse threatens the "literary," the "historical," "women," by insisting on temporality, on shifting relations rather than fixed categories and values.

A melancholy coda. In my university, and in the secondary school curriculum in New England at least, any text from the Renaissance, however marginal, however decentered—ballads, jigs, penny histories, long ignored and forgotten plays—produces "canonical effects." That is, any text from an historical period before the French revolution is construed as "canonical." History itself, mere *pastness*, produces canonical effects. Similarly, the turn to history, however textualized, however problematized or theorized, produces a similar "history effect" that is powerfully conservative and that explains why cultural studies is being institutionalized as the study of contemporary mass culture—not popular culture of the past, only the present, a present that continues to include the nineteenth century so as not to jettison Marx or Freud. Given the commanding force of what I have termed the history effect to construct any cultural production of the past as canonical, is political criticism possible in the Renaissance?

# NOTES

## INTRODUCTION

1. "A Juvenal Quotation Opens the Tower Report," *New York Times*, 1 March 1987.

2. See Joan Scott, "Gender: A Useful Category of Historical Analysis," *Gender and the Politics of History* (New York: Columbia University Press, 1988), esp. 46ff.

3. For a brief account, see Lawrence Stone, *The Causes of the English Revolution 1529–1642* (New York: Harper & Row, 1972), and his *Crisis of the Aristocracy 1558–1641* (Oxford: Clarendon Press, 1965). Though revisionist historians have recently challenged the notion of an English revolution in the 1640s, that enormous economic and demographic change took place is not in dispute. See also Peter Laslett, *The World We Have Lost* (New York: Scribner's, 1965, rpt. 1984). For the historical material in a literary context, see Lisa Jardine, *Still Harping on Daughters* (Sussex: Harvester Press, 1983).

4. David Underdown, "The Taming of the Scold: The Enforcement of Patriarchal Authority in Early Modern England," *Order and Disorder in Early Modern England*, ed. Anthony Fletcher and John Stevenson (Cambridge: Cambridge University Press, 1985), 119.

5. Joan Kelly, *Women, History, and Theory* (Chicago: University of Chicago Press, 1984), 19–50.

6. See Denise Riley, *"Am I That Name?" Feminism and the Category of 'Women' in History* (Minneapolis: University of Minnesota Press, 1988), and Judith Butler, *Gender Trouble: Feminism and the Subversion of Identity* (New York: Routledge, 1990).

7. I assume that gender, race, sexuality, and class are discursive rather than ontological categories. On the discursive construction of gender, for example, see Joan Scott and Judith Butler, cited above; on race, see Barbara Fields, "Ideology and Race in American History," *Region, Race and Reconstruction*, ed. J. Morgan Kousser and James M. McPherson (New York: Oxford University Press, 1982), 143–77 and *Critical Inquiry* 12 (1985); on sexuality, see Jeffrey Weeks, *Sexuality and Its Discontents* (London: Routledge and Kegan Paul, 1985);

on class see E. P. Thompson, "Eighteenth-Century English Society: Class Struggle without Class?" *Social History* 3 (1978), the preface to E. P. Thompson, *The Making of the English Working Class* (New York: Random House, 1966), and Gareth Steadman Jones, *Languages of Class* (Cambridge: Cambridge University Press, 1983).

## CHAPTER 1

1. On woman's relation to the body, see Elizabeth Spelman, "Women as Body: Ancient and Contemporary Views," *Feminist Studies* 8 (1982): 109–31.

2. Elaine Scarry, *The Body in Pain* (New York: Oxford University Press, 1985), 194 ff. Though not my subject here, Scarry's emphasis on Genesis as a story not so much of the fall as of generation, the creation of the world and its populations, is important. Human generation, as witnessed by the Biblical genealogy "carries us back to a time when the duration of a people was more precarious, and when its survival and rapid growth were thus occasions for triumphant recitation," 192. The demographic story of early modern England, the rapid changes in the composition of villages and towns, suggests a similar fragility of generation and its accompanying anxiety. Scarry goes on to analyse the structural distinction in Genesis between the voice of God and the body of man: "The place of man and the place of God in the human generation that so dominates Genesis are easy to separate from one another: the place of man is in the body; the place of God is in the voice," 192.

3. David Cressy, *Literacy and the Social Order: Reading and Writing in Tudor and Stuart England* (Cambridge: Cambridge University Press, 1980).

4. The question of the signature in assessing literacy is discussed by R. S. Schofield, "The Measurement of Literacy in Pre-industrial England," *Literacy in Traditional Societies,* ed. J. R. Goody (Cambridge: Cambridge University Press, 1968), 318–25. On women and the signature, see Alain Derville, "L'alphabétisation du peuple à la fin du moyen âge," *Revue du Nord* 26 (1984): 761–76. On the problem of what constitutes literacy, see Brian Street, *Literacy in Theory and Practice* (Cambridge: Cambridge University Press, 1984).

5. Margaret Spufford, *Small Books and Pleasant Histories: Popular Fiction and Its Readership in Seventeenth-Century England* (Cambridge: Cambridge University Press, 1981), 21ff.

6. Lady Brilliana's letters attest that she apparently conformed to the womanly ideal Gataker describes; *Letters of Lady Brilliana Harley,* ed. Thomas T. Lewis (London, 1854).

7. Thomas Gataker, "A Wife Indeed," *Two Marriage Sermons* (London, 1623), E1$^r$.

8. On the tripartite ideal of chastity, silence and obedience, see Robert Greene's *Penelope's Web* (1587), a series of exemplary tales; Ruth Kelso, *Doctrine for the Lady of the Renaissance* (Urbana: University of Illinois Press, 1956); Linda T. Fitz, "'What Says the Married Woman?': Marriage Theory and Feminism in the English Renaissance," *Mosaic* 13 (1980): 1–22; the books Suzanne Hull examines in her *Chaste, Silent, and Obedient: English Books for Women, 1475–1640* (San Marino, CA: Huntington Library, 1982); and Lisa Jardine, *Still Harping on Daughters* (Sussex: Harvester Press, 1983), 103–40.

9. Henry Smith, *A Preparative to Mariage* (London: 1591), D2$^r$.

10. Thomas Becon, *Workes* (London, 1564), ccc1$^r$, and William Whately, *A Bride-Bush* (London, 1623), Dd3$^r$, Ee2$^r$.

11. Ibid., xx2$^v$.

12. Smith, *A Preparative to Mariage,* D1$^v$, D2$^v$, and repeated in Robert Cleaver's derivative *A Godly Forme of Household Government* (London,1598), H3$^r$ and in the 1630 edition, G4$^r$.

13. Recent examples of review essays that illustrate how woman is produced as victim: Lynda Boose, "The Family in Shakespeare Studies; or—Studies in the Family of Shakespeareans; or—The Politics of Politics," *Renaissance Quarterly* 40 (Winter, 1987), and Judith Lowder Newton, "History as Usual? Feminism and the 'New Historicism,'" *Cultural Critique* (Spring, 1988): 87–121. For a survey of such criticism of Shakespeare, see Carolyn Heilbrun's review in *Signs* 8 (1982): 182–86, but also my comment, *Signs* 10 (1985): 601–3. Perhaps the most powerful articulation of the containment argument is Stephen Greenblatt, "Invisible Bullets: Renaissance Authority and Its Subversion, *Henry IV* and *Henry V,*" *Political Shakespeare,* ed. Jonathan Dollimore and Alan Sinfield (Ithaca: Cornell University Press), 18–47, subsequently reprinted in his *Shakespearean Negotiations* (Berkeley: University of California Press, 1988). Margaret Ferguson's argument that containment theories represent "a political gesture of considerable radical force" in the context of United States ideologies of "free will" brilliantly historicizes the "containment" debate (personal communication), but see also her "Afterword," 276, and Walter Cohen, "Political Criticism of Shakespeare," both in *Shakespeare Reproduced,* ed. Jean Howard and Marion F. O'Connor (New York: Methuen, 1987).

14. "Imaginary" in the sense in which Lacan uses the term and which he opposes to the Symbolic register. See Jacques Lacan, "Le stade du miroir comme formateur de la fonction du Je," *Ecrits I* (Paris: Editions du Seuil, 1966).

15. For challenges to our common sense notions of the body and their significance to feminist work, See Donna Haraway, "A Manifesto for Cyborgs:

Science, Technology, and Socialist Feminism in the 1980s," *Socialist Review* 80 (1985): 65–107.

## CHAPTER 2

1. In *Renaissance Self-Fashioning* (Chicago: University of Chicago Press, 1980), Stephen Greenblatt has written eloquently of the new status of the Bible in Protestant England, of its displacement of "the *consensus fidelium* as the principle of intelligibility and the justification of all action," 99.

2. For an excellent survey and analysis of English and continental conduct books that includes books of courtiership, see Ann Rosalind Jones, "Nets and Bridles: Early Modern Conduct Books and Sixteenth-Century Women's Lyrics," *The Ideology of Conduct,* ed. Nancy Armstrong and Leonard Tennenhouse (New York: Routledge, Chapman & Hall, 1987), 39–72. See also Lisa Jardine, *Still Harping on Daughters* (Sussex: Harvester Press, 1983), chap. 2.

3. Thomas Gataker, *Two Marriage Sermons* (London, 1623), E1[r].

4. John Wing, *The Crowne Conjugall or the Spouse Royall. A Discovery of the Honor and Happines of Christian Matrimony* (London, 1620), P7[r-v].

5. For a description of the organization and significance of the early modern family, see Laslett, *The World We Have Lost* (New York: Harper & Row, 1965, rpt. 1984), 1–21, and Susan Dwyer Amussen, *An Ordered Society. Gender and Class in Early Modern England* (New York: B. Blackwell, 1988); Keith Wrightson, *English Society 1580–1680* (New Brunswick: Rutgers University Press, 1982). On marriage among the elite, see Lawrence Stone, *The Family, Sex, and Marriage in England 1500–1800* (New York: Harper & Row, 1977, rpt. 1979).

6. John Aylmer quoted in Gordon Schochet, *Patriarchalism in Political Thought* (New York: Basic Books, 1975), 45; see also R. W. K. Hinton, "Husbands, Fathers and Conquerors," *Political Studies* 15 (1967): 291–300.

7. For discussion of the way Elizabeth I exploited her sexual difference by presenting herself as an unattainable beloved, see the various essays by Louis Montrose; for Elizabeth's representation of herself androgynously as both Prince and Father, see Leah Marcus, *Puzzling Shakespeare, Local Reading and Its Discontents* (Berkeley: University of California Press, 1988), chap. 2.

8. William Whately, *A Bride-Bush* (London, 1623), x2[r].

9. *Certain Sermons or Homilies (1547) and A Homily Against Disobedience and Wilful Rebellion* (1570), ed. Ronald Bond (Toronto: University of Toronto Press, 1987).

10. What is troubling about Laslett's claim is that he seems to believe therefore that they—women, children, servants—are unfit subjects of histori-

cal analysis. For Laslett the theory of "subsumption" is an attack on marxist, and proleptically, feminist analysis. See *The World We Have Lost,* 20–21.

11. Francis Dillingham, *A Golden Keye Opening the Locke to Eternall Happiness* (London, 1609), I1ʳ.

12. See, for example, William and Malleville Haller, "The Puritan Art of Love," *Huntington Library Quarterly* 5 (1941–42): 235–72; Lawrence Stone, cited above. For an early argument in the context of Shakespeare studies, see Juliet Dusinberre, *Shakespeare and the Nature of Women* (New York: Barnes & Noble, 1975). Kathleen M. Davies summarizes the argument about the effects of Protestantism on women's situation in "The Sacred Condition of Equality—How Original Were Puritan Doctrines of Marriage?" *Social History* 5 (1977): 563–81.

13. See Laslett, cited above.

14. Kathleen M. Davies, "Continuity and Change in Literary Advice on Marriage," *Marriage and Society Studies in the Social History of Marriage,* ed. R. B. Outhwaite (New York: St. Martin's Press, 1981), 59.

15. See also C. L. Powell, *English Domestic Relations 1487–1653: A Study of Matrimony and Family Life in Theory and Practice as Revealed in Literature, Law and History* (New York: Columbia University Press, 1917).

16. Davies does point out that the puritan handbooks differ from earlier advice in suggesting the possibility of divorce and remarriage under certain circumstances and in rejecting the notion that voluntary sexual abstinence by married couples was a means of obtaining grace, "Continuity and Change," 78.

17. Louis Althusser, "Ideology and Ideological State Apparatuses," *Lenin and Philosophy and Other Essays,* tr. Ben Brewster (New York: Monthly Review Press, 1971).

18. O. B. Hardison, Jr., ed. *English Literary Criticism. The Renaissance* (New York: Appleton-Century-Crofts, 1963), 50. On the Renaissance aesthetic of *copia,* see Marion Trousdale, "A Possible Renaissance View of Form," *ELH* 40 (1973): 179–204.

19. On the notion of *heteroglossia,* see M. M. Bakhtin, *The Dialogic Imagination,* trans. Michael Holquist and Caryl Emerson (Austin: University of Texas Press, 1981), 266 ff., and chap. 6 below.

20. For a discussion of Becon's homily, see Ronald B. Bond, "'Dark Deeds Doubly Answered': Thomas Becon's Homily Against Whoredom and Adultery, Its Contexts, and Its Affiliation with Three Shakespearean Plays," *Sixteenth Century Journal* 16 (1985): 191–205.

21. Sidney, who had lodged with Ramus's printer André Wechel in Frankfort, facilitated the dissemination of Ramist works into England and Ireland.

Following being named University Professor of Rhetoric at Cambridge, Gabriel Harvey published an ode in memory of Ramus, who was enormously influential in England, particularly among those with Puritan sympathies at Cambridge. See Walter J. Ong, *Ramus, Method, and the Decay of Dialogue* (Cambridge: Harvard University Press, 1958, rpt. 1983), 302.

22. Neal W. Gilbert, *Renaissance Concepts of Method* (New York: Columbia University Press, 1960).

23. Ong, 9.

24. William Gouge, *Of Domesticall Duties* (London, 1634), 3*[r]

25. Whately's table can be found in earlier editions of *A Bride-Bush* as well. In the 1617 edition, it appears at the end of the text and is entitled simply "The duties of the married people are." Nigel Smith remarks the puritan habit of Ramist binary analysis in his introduction to *A Collection of Ranter Writings from the 17th Century* (London, 1983), 33. For the spatial and visual tyranny of representations of sexual difference, see Luce Irigaray, *Speculum de l'autre femme* (Paris: Editions de Minuit, 1974).

26. Amussen, 3 and passim; Judith Butler, *Gender Trouble: Feminism and the Subversion of Identity* (New York: Routledge, 1990), 18.

27. Jacques Derrida, *Margins of Philosophy*, trans. Alan Bass (Chicago: University of Chicago Press, 1984), 17.

28. Even arguing *in utramque partem*, on both sides of a question, promotes a logic of *copia*, paradoxically perhaps, since in practice such forms of argumentation more often led to multiple than to binary perspectives. Consult Joel Altman, *The Tudor Play of Mind* (Berkeley: University of California Press, 1978).

29. Althusser, "Ideology and Ideological State Apparatuses," 162.

30. Wing, B2[r].

31. For an excellent survey of the evidence of non-elite marriage in the sixteenth and seventeenth centuries, see John R. Gillis, *For Better or Worse: British Marriage, 1600 to the Present* (New York: Oxford University Press, 1985), esp. Part I.

32. David Underdown, "The Taming of the Scold: the enforcement of patriarchal authority in early modern England," *Order and Disorder in Early Modern England*, ed. Anthony Fletcher and John Stevenson (Cambridge: Cambridge University Press, 1985), 116–35.

33. Underdown, 121, citing E. P. Thompson, "'Rough Music': Le Charivari Anglais," *Annales ESC* 27 (1972): 285–312.

34. B. H. Cunnington, "A Skimmington in 1618," *Folk-Lore* 41 (1930):

287–90. I am grateful to David Underdown for this reference and for his advice about this account.

35. Michel Foucault, *The History of Sexuality* (New York: Vintage, 1980), I, 101.

36. Keith Thomas, "Women and the Civil War Sects," *Past and Present* 13 (1958): 42–62; Christopher Hill, *The World Turned Upside Down: Radical Ideas and the English Revolution* (Harmondsworth: Penguin, 1975); Patricia Higgins, "The Reactions of Women, with Special Reference to Women Petitioners," *Politics, Religion and the English Civil War*, ed. Brian Manning (New York: St. Martin's Press, 1973), 177–222; and Walter Cohen, "'None of Woman Born': Shakespeare, Women and Revolution," unpublished typescript, esp. 7–9; and James Holstun, "Ranting at the New Historicism," *English Literary Renaissance*, 19 (1989): 189–225.

37. Quoted in Amussen, 62.

38. On style in radical writing, see Nigel Smith, *Perfection Proclaimed, Language and Literature in English Radical Religion 1640–1660* (Oxford: Clarendon, 1989), esp. chap. 8.

39. For the legal perspective, see George Elliott Howard, *History of Matrimonial Institutions* (New York: Humanities Press, 1964), 2: 76–85; Stone, 37–41; and Catherine Belsey, "Alice Arden's Crime," *Renaissance Drama* 13 (1982): 83–102.

CHAPTER 3

1. This would seem to be Rosyer's neighbor's duty. The *Oxford English Dictionary* cites Lupton's *Sivgila*, 50 (1580), as an early use of cowlstaff: "If a woman beat hir husbande, the man that dwell next unto hir sha ride a cowlstaff." Thomas Platter claimed a neighbor rode cowlstaff dressed as a woman as a punishment for failing to assist the husband being beaten. Certainly Quarry seems more perpetrator than victim here. See *Thomas Platter's Travels in England, 1599*, trans. Clare Williams (London: Cape, 1937), 182.

2. PRO STAC 8, 249/19. I am grateful to Susan Amussen for sharing her transcription of this case and to David Underdown for the original reference. The result of Rosyer's complaint is unknown; only the testimony, not the judgment, is preserved.

3. Louis Montrose, "'Shaping Fantasies': Gender and Power in Elizabethan Culture," *Representations* 1 (1983): 61–94.

4. See Natalie Zemon Davis, "Women on Top," in *Society and Culture in Early*

*Modern France* (Stanford: Stanford University Press, 1975); E. P. Thompson, "'Rough Music': le Charivari Anglais," *Annales ESC* 27 (1972): 285–312.

5. In *The Taming of a Shrew* the frame tale closes the action; Sly must return home after his "bravest dreame" to a wife who "will course you for dreaming here tonight," but he claims: "Ile to my/Wife presently and tame her too." See Geoffrey Bullough, Narrative and Dramatic Sources of Shakespeare (London: Routledge and Kegan Paul, 1957), I,: 108.

6. See Montrose's discussion of the Amazonian myth in "Shaping Fantasies," 66–67.

7. Fredric Jameson, *The Political Unconscious* (Ithaca: Cornell University Press, 1981), 35.

8. (I, i, 157–58); all references are to the Arden edition, ed. Brian Morris (London: Methuen, 1981).

9. See chapter 2, above.

10. See, among others, Lawrence Stone, *The Crisis of the Aristocracy 1558–1680* (Oxford: Oxford University Press, 1965) and Keith Wrightson, *English Society 1580–1680* (New Brunswick: Rutgers University Press, 1982), esp. chaps. 5 and 6.

11. David Underdown, "The Taming of the Scold: the enforcement of patriarchal authority in Early Modern England," *Order and Disorder in Early Modern England,* ed. Anthony Fletcher and John Stevenson (Cambridge: Cambridge University Press, 1985), 116–36.

12. See Introduction, above, xviii.

13. Underdown, 120.

14. Underdown, 121, citing E. P. Thompson.

15. Montrose, 64–65.

16. Montrose, 64–65. See also Davis and Thompson, cited above.

17. E.g., I, i, 65, 105, 121, 123; II, i, 26, 151; on gender and witchcraft, see chapter 4, below; for the social context of English witchcraft, see Alan Macfarlane, *Witchcraft in Tudor and Stuart England* (New York: Harper & Row, 1970) and Keith Thomas, *Religion and the Decline of Magic* (London: Weidenfeld & Nicolson, 1971).

18. For carting as a means of social control, see Robert Ashton, "Popular Entertainment and Social Control in Later Elizabethan and Jacobean England," *The London Journal* 9 (1983): 13–15. On the importance of the gaze in managing human behavior, see Michel Foucault, *Surveiller et Punir* (Paris: Gallimard, 1975) and Irigaray, *Speculum de l'autre femme* (Paris: Editions de

Minuit, 1974); see also Laura Mulvey's discussion of scopophilia in "Visual Pleasure and Narrative Cinema," *Screen* 16 (1975): 6–18.

19. Kate's speech at III, ii, makes clear this function of his lateness and his "mad-brain rudesby." She recognizes that shame falls not on her family, but on her alone: "No shame but mine.../Now must the world point at poor Katherine/And say, 'Lo, there is mad Petruchio's wife,/If it would please him come and marry her'" (8, 18–20). Although Katherine to herself, she recognizes that for others she is already "Petruchio's wife."

20. See Marianne Novy's discussion of the importance of the father and paternity, "Patriarchy and Play in *The Taming of the Shrew*," *English Literary Renaissance* 9 (1979): 273–74.

21. Underdown, 120.

22. See Novy's detailed discussion of Kate's puns, animal imagery, and sexual innuendoes in this scene, 264, and Martha Andreson-Thom's "Shrew-taming and Other Rituals of Aggression: Baiting and Bonding on the Stage and in the Wild," *Women's Studies* 9 (1982): 121–43.

23. Sigmund Freud, *Collected Papers*, tr. Joan Rivière (London: International Psychoanalytic Press, 1948), II, 51–59.

24. Freud, II, 51.

25. For a discussion of female fantasy, see Nancy K. Miller, "Emphasis Added? Plots and Plausibilities in Women's Fiction," *PMLA* 97 (1981): 36–48.

26. Freud, II, 57.

27. Freud, II, 58.

28. See Joan Rivière's essay on female masquerade in *Psychoanalysis and Female Sexuality*, ed. H. Ruitenbeek (New Haven: Yale University Press, 1966); also of interest is Sir Thomas Elyot's *Defense of Good Women* in which Zenobia is allowed autonomy in relation to her husband but exhorted to dissemble her disobedience; Constance Jordan, "Feminism and the Humanists: The Case of Thomas Elyot's *Defence of Good Women*," *Renaissance Quarterly* 36 (1983): 195.

29. Freud describes a similar strategy of evasion in II, 58.

30. John Bean, "Comic Structure and the Humanizing of Kate in *The Taming of the Shrew*," in *The Woman's Part*, ed. Carolyn Ruth Swift Lenz, Gayle Greene, and Carol Thomas Neely (Urbana: University of Illinois Press, 1980).

31. Bean, 66.

32. Ibid., 67–70.

33. See Nancy K. Miller's discussion of the mystification of defloration and marriage in "Writing (from) the Feminine: George Sand and the Novel of

Female Pastoral," in *The Representation of Women: English Institute Essays* (Baltimore: Johns Hopkins University Press, 1983), 125–51.

34. Luce Irigaray, *Ce sexe qui n' en est pas un* (Paris: Editions de Minuit, 1977), 134ff. Also available in English translation, *This Sex Which Is Not One*, trans. Catherine Porter with Carolyn Burke (Ithaca: Cornell University Press, 1985).

35. Irigaray, *Speculum de l'autre femme,* particularly 282–98.

36. Irigaray, *Ce sexe,* 74, quoted and translated by Nancy Miller, "Emphasis Added?" 38.

37. Miller, "Emphasis Added?" 38.

38. Joel Fineman, "The Turn of the *Shrew*," in *Shakespeare and the Question of Theory,* ed. Patricia Parker and Geoffrey Hartman (London: Methuen, 1985), 141–44.

39. D. A. Miller in his discussion of Jane Austen describes the "narratable" in *Narrative and Its Discontents* (Princeton: Princeton University Press, 1981).

40. Jameson, 79, 56.

41. For the anthropological argument, see Barbara Babcock, ed., *The Reversible World: Symbolic Inversion in Art and Society* (Ithaca: Cornell University Press, 1978), 13–36, and more recently, Peter Stallybrass and Allon White, *The Politics and Poetics of Transgression* (London: Methuen, 1986). For a brief survey of the educational theorists, see Margaret Ferguson, "Afterword," in *Shakespeare Reproduced,* ed. Jean E. Howard and Marion F. O'Connor (New York: Methuen, 1987), 273–83.

42. Jonathan Dollimore, *Radical Tragedy* (Chicago: University of Chicago Press, 1984), 61.


CHAPTER 4

1. Both Peter Stallybrass, "*Macbeth* and Witchcraft," in *Focus on Macbeth,* ed. J. R. Brown (London: Routledge and Kegan Paul, 1982) and Janet Adelman, "'Born of Woman': Fantasies of Maternal Power in *Macbeth*," in *Cannibals, Witches, and Divorce,* ed. Marjorie Garber, *Selected Papers From the English Institute, 1985* 11 (Baltimore: Johns Hopkins University Press, 1987), note the links between Lady Macbeth and the witches.

2. Quoted by Keith Thomas, *Religion and the Decline of Magic* (London: Weidenfeld and Nicolson, 1971), 445.

3. Alan Macfarlane, *Witchcraft in Tudor and Stuart England: A Regional and Comparative Study* (London: Routledge and Kegan Paul, 1970), 16.

4. Christina Larner, *Witchcraft and Religion* (Oxford: Blackwell, 1984), 36.

5. See H. R. Trevor-Roper, *Religion, the Reformation and Social Change* (London: Macmillan, 1967).

6. See Thomas and Macfarlane, cited above.

7. Gifford, *Discourse of the Subtill Practices of Devilles by Witches and Sorcerers* (1587), G4$^r$–G4$^v$.

8. On labeling and deviance, see Jack Katz, "Deviance, Charisma and Rule-Defined Behavior," *Social Problems* 20 (1972): 186–202, and John Hagan, "Labelling and Deviance: A Case Study in the 'Sociology of the Interesting,'" *Social Problems* 20 (1973): 447–458.

9. Statistically men were much more likely to be "good" witches: cunning men and healers; see Thomas and Macfarlane.

10. Reginald Scot, *The Discoverie of Witchcraft*, ed. Montague Summers (London: J. Rodker, 1930).

11. Important exceptions include Christina Larner, cited above, and Joseph Klaits, *Servants of Satan* (Bloomington: Indiana University Press, 1985). Also worth noting is the work of scholars arguing that accusations of witchcraft stem from the emerging professionalization and accompanying masculinization of medicine. See Thomas Rogers Forbes, *The Midwife and the Witch* (New Haven: Yale, 1966), and Barbara Ehrenreich and Dierdre English, *Witches, Midwives and Nurses* (New York: Feminist Press, 1973). For a review of the relation between women and witchcraft, see Clarke Garrett, "Women and Witches: Patterns of Analysis," *Signs* 3 (1977): 461–70.

12. Larner, 84–85.

13. *The Dramatic Works of Thomas Dekker,* ed. Fredson Bowers (Cambridge: Cambridge University Press, 1958), III. All references are to this edition.

14. Larner, 25.

15. Jacques Derrida, "Signature event context," *Margins of Philosophy*, tr. Alan Bass (Chicago: University of Chicago Press, 1982), 310.

16. In his important essay "Inversion, Misrule and the Meaning of Witchcraft," *Past and Present* 87 (1980): 98–127, Stuart Clark argues that witchcraft was a version of the world turned upside down that Natalie Davis and other historians of the early modern period have shown to be so significant a part of the social formation and politics of early modern Europe. Clark describes how what witches are said to do was an inversion of order, including the use of certain rituals and rhetorical forms; but he overlooks the narrative of inverted motherhood.

17. Boose, "The Family in Shakespeare Studies; or—Studies in the Family

of Shakespeareans; or—The Politics of Politics," *Renaissance Quarterly* 40 (Winter, 1987): 714.

18. Sigmund Freud, *Three Essays on the Theory of Sexuality,* trans. and ed. James Strachey (New York: Basic Books, 1962), 47.

19. Melanie Klein, "Weaning," in *On the Bringing Up of Children,* ed. John Rickman (London: Kegan Paul, Trench, Trubner & Co., 1936), 32–33.

20. John Gaule, "A True Relation of the Araignment of eighteene Witches at St. Edmundsbury..." (London, 1645), 9. Searchers were instructed to "take the partie or parties so suspected into a Roome and strip him, her, or them, starke naked." Also quoted in Wallace Notestein, *A History of Witchcraft in England* (New York: Russell & Russell, 1911, rpt. 1965), 174–75.

21. For a full transcript, see Peter Haining, *The Witchcraft Papers* (Seacacus, N. J.: University Books, 1974).

22. Notestein records many such cases; see also Haining, and cases recounted in Joseph H. Marshburn, *Murder & Witchcraft in England, 1550–1640* (Norman: University of Oklahoma Press, 1971).

23. Harry Berger, "The Early Scenes of *Macbeth*: Preface to a New Interpretation," *ELH* 47 (1980): 1.

24. Witness the *New York Times*'s recent publication, on its front page immediately beneath the little box and motto, "All the News That's Fit to Print," of an article entitled "Female Sex Hormone is Tied to Ability to Perform Tasks," in which the results of a study were supported by a minuscule sample subject to myriad interpretations having nothing to do with hormones (18 November 1988). For the problems of "scientific" explanations of sexual difference, see Anne Fausto-Sterling's *Myths of Gender* (New York: Basic Books, 1984).

25. In her recent *The Mother/Daughter Plot* (Bloomington: Indiana University Press, 1989), Marianne Hirsch argues within a psychoanalytic frame for the importance of historicizing the terms "mother" and "motherhood."

26. In Renaissance studies, history and psychoanalysis have recently been pitted against one another as an irreconcilable binarism that in turn generates within the profession a series of binary oppositions: public/private, state/family, theory/interpretation, and last but not least, men/women. See, for example, Boose, cited n. 17 above.

27. Jean Laplanche, *Life and Death in Psychoanalysis,* tr. Jeffrey Mehlman (Baltimore: Johns Hopkins University Press, 1976), 15ff. French rereadings of Freud have by and large not been taken up by feminist critics of Shakespeare in the United States. Boose claims that "having refurbished psychoanalytic

usage with its missing maternal pole, [they] were perhaps disinclined to return to 'the Law of the Father' (Lacan)" (715).

28. Sigmund Freud, *The Origins of Psycho-analysis*, ed. Marie Bonaparte, Anna Freud, and Ernst Kris; trans. Eric Mosbacher and James Strachey (New York: Basic Books, 1954), 187.

29. *The (M)other Tongue*, ed. Shirley Nelson Garner, Claire Kahane and Madelon Sprengnether (Ithaca: Cornell University Press, 1985), 358.

30. Derrida, "Signature event context," 320.

31. For an elegant Derridean account of *Macbeth* to which I am indebted, see Jonathan Goldberg, "Speculations: *Macbeth* and Source," in *Shakespeare Reproduced*, ed. Jean Howard and Marion F. O'Connor (New York: Methuen, 1987), 242–64.

32. Geoffrey Bullough, ed., *Narrative and Dramatic Sources of Shakespeare* (London: Routledge and Kegan Paul, 1973), VII, 479–80.

33. The supernatural powers of mimesis might also be useful: cunning men and women engaged in what was termed *specularii*, the practice of looking into a mirror to discover thieves or the whereabouts of lost objects.

34. Arguments for the execution of witches were based on scriptural exegesis, the translation and interpretation of the Latin "Veneficam non retinebitis in vita," the translation of which was argued and debated: did it mean "you shall not suffer a witch to live," or alternatively, did *veneficam* mean poisoner; and what, if any, is the relation between that interpretation and those termed witches in Elizabethan England?

35. See Stephen Greenblatt's reading of Harsnett's *Declaration* in *Shakespearean Negotiations* (Berkeley: University of California Press, 1988), particularly his argument that possession "depended upon an interpretive supplement," 109.

36. See Haining, cited above, for a full transcript of the Waterhouse examination and trial, and Notestein, 40, who also refers to other cases of witches speaking Latin. See also Henry Goodcole, *The wonderful discoverie of Elizabeth Sawyer, A witch, late of Edmonton...*(London, 1621), the pamphlet that inspired Dekker, Rowley and Ford's play, which dramatizes the devil's teaching Mother Sawyer Latin spells (II, i, 170ff.).

37. Thomas notes the relation between religous opposition and witchcraft and sorcery when he observes that under Elizabeth I *conjuror* was a synonym for recusant priest, 68. Similarly, "Sathan" may be a stand-in for the Pope and thus a disclaimer of responsibility for the resistance of the papist Latin prayer (Stephen Greenblatt, personal communication).

38. Stephen Greenblatt, *Shakespearean Negotiations* (Berkeley: University of California Press, 1988), 96.

39. Catherine Belsey, *The Subject of Tragedy* (London: Methuen, 1985), 190–91.

40. Quoted in Frank L. Huntley, "*Macbeth* and the Background of Jesuitical Equivocation," *PMLA* 79 (1964): 390. Huntley takes the example from a defense of equivocation by Robert Parsons, S.J., addressed to Thomas Morton, Bishop of Durham.

41. "Equivocation" has played many parts in *Macbeth* criticism. Scholars date the play subsequent to the trial and execution of Father Garnett and the Gunpowder Plot; Warburton glossed the Porter's term "equivocator" as "a Jesuit; an order so troublesome in Queen Elizabeth's and King James the First's time"; commentators have since thematized the topical reference as "appearance and reality." More recently it has been discussed as "amphibology" and associated once more with treason; see Steven Mullaney, *The Place of the Stage* (Chicago: University of Chicago Press, 1988).

42. Jacques Derrida, "Sending: On Representation," trans. Mary Ann and Peter Caws, *Social Research* 49 (1982): 309.

43. Stanley Cavell, "Epistemology and Tragedy: A Reading of *Othello*," *Daedalus* 108 (1979): 43.

CHAPTER 5

1. Thomas Rymer, "A Short View of Tragedy," *Critical Essays of the Seventeenth Century*, ed. J. E. Spingarn (Bloomington, Indiana University Press, 1957), II, 221–22.

2. S. T. Coleridge, *Shakespearean Criticism*, ed. Thomas M. Raysor (London, 1960), 42.

3. M. R. Ridley, ed., *Othello* (London: Methuen, 1958, rpt. 1984), li. All references are to this edition.

4. On the racism of commentators, see Martin Orkin, "*Othello* and the 'plain face' of Racism," *Shakespeare Quarterly* 38 (1987): 166–88. Orkin points out that Ridley's edition is the preferred text in South Africa.

5. For a useful general discussion of black and white and their cultural associations, see the opening chapter of Harry Levin, *The Power of Blackness* (New York: Vintage, 1958). On *Othello*, see Doris Adler, "The Rhetoric of *Black* and *White* in *Othello*," *Shakespeare Quarterly* 25 (1974): 248–57.

6. Winthrop Jordan, *White over Black* (Chapel Hill: University of North Carolina Press, 1968), 7.

7. Stephen Orgel, *The Jonsonian Masque* (Cambridge: Harvard University Press, 1967; rpt. New York: Columbia University Press, 1981), 120.

a. Whitney chose the woodcuts from a collection of Christopher Plantyn, the well-known printer whose shop published *A Choice of Emblemes;* see Charles H. Lyons, *To Wash an Aethiop White: British Ideas about African Educability 1530–1960* (New York: Teacher's College Press, 1975), iv–v.

b. For references to this phrase in Elizabethan and Jacobean drama, see Robert R. Cawley, *The Voyages and Elizabethan Drama* (Boston: D. C. Heath, 1938), 85ff.

c. E. V. Lucas, *Highways and Byways in Sussex* (London, 1904), my emphasis; I am grateful to Peter Stallybrass for this reference.

8. For a general account of the classical materials, see Frank M. Snowden, Jr., *Before Color Prejudice* (Cambridge: Harvard University Press, 1983).

9. All the passages quoted appear in R. Hakluyt, *The Principal Navigations, Voyages Traffiques & Discoveries of the English Nation* (1600), ed. Walter Raleigh (Glasgow, 1903–5), VII, 262. Best's *Discourse* was reprinted in a substantially cut version. The story of the origins of blackness in Noah's son Cham is also found in Leo Africanus's popular *Historie of Africa* (1526).

10. Jordan observes that "English experience was markedly different from that of the Spanish and Portuguese who, for centuries, had been in close contact with North Africa and had actually been invaded and subjected by people both darker and more highly civilized than themselves....One of the fairest skinned nations suddenly came face to face with one of the darkest peoples on earth" (6).

11. Hakluyt's book is said to have been a prime motivator of English colonial expansion and to have increased the profits of the East India Company by some twenty thousand pounds; see Walter Raleigh's introductory essay, I, 92.

12. Talmudic and Midrashic commentaries, which inspired interest in the humanist sixteenth century, seem to have been the source for the link between blackness and the curse on Cham; see Jordan, 17–20; 35–39.

13. Jacques Derrida, "Racism's Last Word," trans. Peggy Kamuf, *Critical Inquiry* 12 (1985): 290–99.

14. Frank Whigham, "Courtesy as a Social Code," *Spenser Encyclopedia*, ed. A.C. Hamilton (Toronto: University of Toronto Press,1990) and also his *Ambition and Privilege* (Berkeley: University of California Press, 1984).

15. *Acts of the Privy Council,* ed. John Roche Dasent (London, 1902), 11 and 18 July, 1596; new series, XXVI, 16, 20). These proclamations must be read in

light of the similar dislike and resentment, based on economic distinctions, between the English and the Fleming and Huguenot clothworkers who fled religious persecution and immigrated to England. The clothworkers, however, not only brought needed skills, they were also European, more like the English than the African could ever be; and though they generated hostility, there is no evidence of similar legislation to oust them from England. See C. W. Chitty, "Aliens in England in the Sixteenth Century," *Race* 8 (1966): 129–145, and Anthony Barker, *The African Link* (London: F. Cass, 1978), 30.

16. Paul L. Hughes and James F. Larkin, eds., *Tudor Royal Proclamations* (New Haven: Yale University Press, 1969), III, 221.

17. Rudolph Wittkower, "Marvels of the East: A Study in the History of Monsters," *Journal of the Warburg and Courtauld Institutes* 5 (1942): 159–97, provides a thorough review, particularly of the visual material. Mary Louise Pratt, "Scratches on the Face of the Country; or, What Mr. Barrow Saw in the Land of the Bushmen," *Critical Inquiry* 12 (1985): 119–43, analyzes two modes of travel writing, the scientific-informational and the subject-centered, experiential, that are suggestive not only for her nineteenth-century texts but for earlier examples that already manifest signs of the distinctions she draws.

18. Though these accounts are strikingly similar to discourses about the New World, comparison would require another study.

19. See among others, John Lok's *Second Voyage to Guinea* (1554), in Hakluyt, VI, 154–77; William Towerson's voyage, 1556–57, Hakluyt, VI, 177–212; George Fenner's voyage, 1556, Hakluyt, VI, 266–84; and finally Richard Jobson, *The Golden Trade* (1623), ed. Walter Rodney (London: Dawsons, 1968), 65–67. Lok's long and interesting account also appeared in the 1589 edition of Hakluyt as Robert Gainsh's voyage.

20. This passage appears only in the Latin *De Republica libri sex* (1601); the translation is Richard Knolles's (London, 1606), available in a facsimile edition, J. Bodin, *The Six Books of a Commonweale,* ed. Kenneth Douglas McRae (Cambridge: Harvard University Press, 1962), Bk. III, viii, 387). The Latin, though somewhat more readable than Knolles's prose, includes both parenthesis and extended subordination (J. Bodini, 1601, L1, 8). Knolles is quoted in David B. Davis, *The Problem of Slavery in Western Culture* (Ithaca: Cornell University Press, 1966), 112.

21. For a review of Portuguese and Spanish sources, see Katherine George, "The Civilized West Looks at Primitive Africa: 1400–1800," *Isis* 49 (1958): 62–72. For a general view of Elizabethans and foreigners, see G. K. Hunter, "Elizabethans and Foreigners," *Shakespeare Survey* 17 (1964): 37–52. On the representation of blacks on the English stage, see Eldred Jones, *Othello's Countrymen:*

*The African in English Renaissance Drama* (London: Oxford University Press, 1965); G. K. Hunter, "*Othello* and Colour Prejudice," *Proceedings of the British Academy* 53 (1967): 139–63; and more recently, Elliot H. Tokson, *The Popular Image of the Black Man in English Drama 1588–1688* (Boston: G. K. Hall, 1982).

22. Keith Thomas, *Religion and the Decline of Magic*, (London: Weidenfeld & Nicolson, 1971), 129.

23. Quoted from R. Burton, *Admirable Curiosities* (1703) in Hyder Rollins, "An Analytical Index of the Ballad Entries in the Registers of the Stationers of London," *Studies in Philology* 21 (1924): 53. Teratological treatises often attributed monstrous births to the maternal imagination and desire, linking femininity to the production of monsters. As Marie-Hélène Huet observes, the "monster publicly signals all aberrant desire, reproves all excessive passion and all illegitimate fantasy"; "Living Images: Monstrosity and Representation," *Representations* 4 (1983): 74. A contemporary English source specifically for the link between the maternal imagination and blackness is Sir Thomas Browne's *Pseudodoxia Epidemica* (1646). Ernest Martin, *Histoires des monstres* (Paris: C. Reinwald, 1880), traces the theory of monstrosity and the maternal imagination, 266–94.

24. Kenneth Burke, *A Grammar of Motives* (Berkeley: University of California Press, 1969) quoted by Stephen Greenblatt in *Renaissance Self-Fashioning*, (Chicago: University of Chicago Press, 1980), 306. Recently, Eve Kosofsky Sedgwick has deconstructed for an Anglo-American audience such versions of "consubstantiality" by showing how the female body, at once desired object and subject of discourse, becomes the territory across which male bonds she terms homosocial are forged between men; see *Between Men: English Literature and Homosocial Desire* (New York: Columbia University Press, 1985.

25. Greenblatt, 245.

26. The Folio reading "traveler's history," with its generic implications, as Greenblatt notes, seems more convincing than "travel's history," since the tale Othello tells is drawn from accounts such as Mandeville's and repeated by the early Elizabethan travelers recorded in Hakluyt.

27. Linda Williams's essay on the horror film motivated a part of this discussion; "When the Woman Looks," *Re-vision: Essays in Feminist Film Criticism*, ed. Mary Ann Doane, Patricia Mellencamp and Linda Williams (Frederick, MD: University Publications of America, 1984).

28. Homi Bhabha's notion of hybridity, which he defines as "the revaluation of the assumption of colonial identity through the repetition of discriminatory identity effects," is suggestive for my reading of *Othello;* "Signs Taken for Wonders: Questions of Ambivalence and Authority Under a Tree Outside

Delhi, May 1817," *Critical Inquiry* 12 (1985): 154. See also his discussion of the colonial subject and mimicry in "Of Mimicry and Man: The Ambivalence of Colonial Discourse," *October* 25 (1983): 125–33, particularly observations about the ambivalence of mimicry as "almost the same, *but not quite*," 127.

29. Bernard Spivack, *The Allegory of Evil* (New York: Columbia University Press, 1958), 415ff.

30. Casual assumptions about the Shakespearean audience are problematic and the "we" of my own critical discourse equally so. Shakespeare's audience was not a classless, genderless monolith. The female spectators at a Globe performance, both the whores in the pit and the good English wives Stephen Gosson chastises for their attendance at the theatre in *The Schoole of Abuse,* view the play from different perspectives from that of a white male audience of whatever social and economic station. As women, if we are implicated in Iago's perspective and Othello's tragedy, we are unsexed, positioned as men; if we identify with Desdemona, we are punished. See the interesting work on female spectatorship in film theory by Laura Mulvey, "Visual Pleasure and Narrative Cinema," *Screen* 16 (1975): 6–18, and Mary Ann Doane, "Film and the Masquerade: Theorizing Female Spectatorship," *Screen* 23 (1983): 74–87.

31. In Leo Africanus's *Historie of Africa* (1526), the "Portugals" are most often singled out as the destroyers of Africa and her peoples. From this perspective, the Iberian origins of Iago's name suggest that his destruction of Othello/Africa can be read as an allegory of colonialism. For detailed, if occasionally dubious, parallels between Leo's *Historie* and *Othello,* see Rosalind Johnson, "African Presence in Shakespearean Drama: *Othello* and Leo Africanus's *Historie of Africa,*" *African Presence in Early Europe,* special issue of the *Journal of African Civilizations* 7 (1985): 267–287.

32. For a recent attempt to look at both race and gender in *Othello,* see Ania Loomba, *Gender, Race, Renaissance Drama* (Manchester: Manchester University Press, 1989), chap. 2.

33. Compare Thomas Becon's lively description of the whore in his "Catechisme," quoted above p. 10. Becon makes explicit what is only implied in *Othello,* the link between female orifices—ear, mouth, genitals—as well as their perceived voraciousness.

34. This alternative sexual economy suggests another trajectory of desire in *Othello* between Iago and Othello, which cannot be explored further here other than to note Iago's repeated au/oral seduction, as for example when he pours "pestilence into his [Othello's] ear" (II, iii, 347). For an interesting discussion of *Othello* and the "pathological male animus toward sexuality," par-

ticularly Desdemona's, see Edward A. Snow, "Sexual Anxiety and the Male Order of Things in *Othello*," *English Literary Renaissance* 10 (1980): 388.

35. I am grateful to Rey Chow and the other members of the Brown Seminar "Cultural Constructions of Gender" (1988) at the Pembroke Center for Teaching and Research on Women for valuable discussion of the play's sexual economies.

36. Quoted by Rymer (1693), ed. Spingarn, 221. On the status of blacks and moors in Renaissance Venice, see Giorgio Fedalto, "Stranieri a Venezia e a Padova," *Storia del cultura veneta dal primo quattrocento al concilio di Trento*, ed. Arnaldi and M. P. Stocchi (Vicenza, 1976), 499–535.

37. For an excellent discussion of gender and class in *Othello*, see Peter Stallybrass, "Patriarchal Territories: The Body Enclosed," *Rewriting the Renaissance*, eds. Margaret Ferguson, Maureen Quilligan, and Nancy Vickers (Chicago: University of Chicago Press, 1986).

38. For a psychoanalytic reading of Othello's relation to "the voice of the father," see Snow, 409–10, cited above.

39. Tony Bennett, "Text and History," *Re-reading English*, ed. Peter Widdowson (London: Methuen, 1982), 229.

40. Quoted in Jordan, 28.

41. James Walvin, *The Black Presence* (New York: Schocken Books, 1972), 13, and Folarin Shyllon, *Black People in Britain 1555–1833* (London: Oxford University Press, 1977). It is worth noting that slavery between Europe and Africa was reciprocal. W. E. B. DuBois points out that during the sixteenth century "the [black] Mohammaden rulers of Egypt were buying white slaves by the tens of thousands in Europe and Asia"; *The World and Africa* (New York: International Publishers, 1972), 111. Blonde women were apparently in special demand. See also Wayne B. Chandler, who points out that "moors" were black, and historians' efforts to claim their tawniness represent racial prejudice; "The Moor: Light of Europe's Dark Age," *African Presence in Early Europe*, special issue of *Journal of African Civilizations* 7 (1985): 144–75.

42. Postlewayt writes in order to justify the Royal African Company's attempts to regain its monopoly; his pamphlet is exemplary, but many others could also be cited. Quoted in Walvin, 51–52.

43. Rymer's attack on Shakespeare in an age of growing Shakespeare idolatry prompted other critics to a different tack, to dispute Othello's blackness altogether rather than reprehend it.

44. This same slippage from blackness to femininity is implicit in the

commonly believed notion that apes and negroes copulated and especially that "apes were inclined wantonly to attack Negro women," Jordan, 31.

45. Rymer, ed. Spingarn, 221.

46. Rymer, ed. Spingarn, 251, 254.

47. Rymer's characterization of Emilia as "the meanest woman in the Play" (254) requires comment. The moralism of the "Short View" might lead most readers to award Bianca that superlative, but predictably Rymer cannot forgive Emilia her spunky cynicism toward men and her defense of women.

48. Norbert Elias, *The Civilizing Process: The History of Manners,* trans. Edmund Jephcott (New York: Urizen Press, 1978), 143–52.

49. Guido Ruggiero, *The Boundaries of Eros: Sex Crimes in Renaissance Venice* (New York: Oxford University Press, 1985), 61–62. I am grateful to Jonathan Goldberg for this reference.

50. See also Stallybrass, cited above.

51. Lawrence Ross, "The Meaning of Strawberries in Shakespeare," *Studies in the Renaissance* 7 (1960): 225–40.

52. Lynda Boose argues that the handkerchief represents the lovers' consummated marriage and wedding sheets stained with blood, a sign of Desdemona's sexual innocence. She links the handkerchief to the folk custom of displaying the spotted wedding sheets as a proof of the bride's virginity; "Othello's Handkerchief: The Recognizance and Pledge of Love," *English Literary Renaissance* 5 (1975): 360–74.

53. Sigmund Freud, "Fetishism" (1927), in *Sexuality and the Psychology of Love,* ed. Phillip Rieff (New York: Macmillan, 1963, rpt. 1978), 215, 216.

54. See, for example, *Othello* I, iii, 402; III, iii, 111, 433.

55. Snow associates the spotted "napkin" not only with Desdemona's stained wedding sheets but also with menstrual blood. He argues that the handkerchief is therefore "a nexus for three aspects of woman—chaste bride, sexual object, and maternal threat" (392).

56. For a discussion of critical attitudes toward Desdemona, and particularly this line, see S. N. Garner, "Shakespeare's Desdemona," *Shakespeare Studies* 9 (1976): 232–52.

57. Greenblatt, 244.

CHAPTER 6

1. R. Hakluyt, *The Principal Navigations, Voyages Traffiques & Discoveries of the English Nation* (1600), ed. Walter Raleigh (Glasgow, 1903–5), VII, 306–7.

2. Steven Mullaney, "Strange Things, Gross Terms, Curious Customs: The Rehearsal of Cultures in the Late Renaissance," *Representations* 3 (1983): 40–67. We know from other records that these two "Eskimos" eventually did "use as man & wife" because a child was born to the couple in England.

3. See Mullaney's *The Place of the Stage* (Chicago: University of Chicago Press, 1988), 82.

4. In Bakhtin's formulation, *heteroglossia* is only possible in the novel and certain other genres from which it developed because of the dialogic organization of novelistic discourse, the presence of an authorial or narrative voice in dialogic relation to the many-voicedness of characters and genres. In drama, Bakhtin complains, "there is no all-encompassing language that addresses itself dialogically to separate languages, there is no second plotless (nondramatic) dialogue outside that of the (dramatic) plot." Though the dramatic immediacy of theatrical representation obscures the fact that the audience watches a constructed world, theatrical representation on the Elizabethan and Jacobean stage, so different from the naturalistic "fourth wall" bourgeois theatre that Bakhtin seems to have in mind, provides a formal equivalent to an authorial voice, to a narrator, and particularly in *Henry V* with its choral preludes that remind the audience of the conventions of theatre. The conventions of the Elizabethan theatre, including acting styles, transvestism, prominent use of rhetoric and of micro-generic intrusions—from the novella to letter writing—establish a dialogic relation with the characters' voices and prevent what Bakhtin calls the domination of "unitary language." M. M. Bakhtin, *The Dialogic Imagination,* tr. Michael Holquist and Caryl Emerson (Austin: University of Texas Press, 1981), 266.

5. Bakhtin, 272.

6. M. A. K. Halliday, *Language as Social Semiotic* (London: Edward Arnold, 1978), 35.

7. J. H. Walter, ed., *Henry V* (London: Methuen, 1954, rpt. 1984), IV, i, 250–55. All references are to this edition, which relies primarily on the Folio text.

8. See, for example, Norman Rabkin, *Shakespeare and the Problem of Meaning* (Chicago: University of Chicago Press, 1981), 33–62. But as Stephen Greenblatt observes, "the very doubts that Shakespeare raises serve not to rob the king of his charisma but to heighten it, precisely as they heighten the theatrical interest of the play....prodded by constant reminders of a gap between real and ideal, facts and values, the spectators are induced to make up the difference, to invest in the illusion of magnificence, to be dazzled by their own imaginary identification with the conqueror"; "Invisible Bullets: Renais-

sance authority and its subversions, *Henry IV* and *Henry V*," in *Political Shakespeare*, ed. Jonathan Dollimore and Alan Sinfield (London: Methuen, 1985), 43. Greenblatt assumes too easily this imaginary "identification with the conqueror," thereby ruling out contestatory voices and producing a monolithic audience, marked here by the definite article—ungendered, unclassed. The female spectator is faced either with a kind of specular masquerade in which she dons a masculine subject position and identifies with the conqueror, or alternatively, masochistic identification with the doubly subject Katherine, woman and synechdochic representative of a conquered France.

9. Cited in Jonathan Dollimore and Alan Sinfield, "History and Ideology: The Instance of *Henry V*," *Alternative Shakespeares*, ed. John Drakakis (London: Methuen, 1985), 224.

10. Dollimore and Sinfield, "History and Ideology," 226.

11. Rowe emended the Folio's "desire" to "defile," which Walter accepts in the Arden edition. Though "defile" is, of course, consistent with "dash'd" and "spitted," the Folio's "desire" stresses the sexual violence against women I am emphasizing here.

12. Mullaney, "Strange Things," 87.

13. Nancy Vickers, "Diana Described: Scattered Woman and Scattered Rhyme," *Critical Inquiry* 8 (1981): 265–80.

14. Laura Mulvey, "Visual Pleasure and Narrative Cinema," *Screen* 16 (1975): 6–18; Paul Willemen, "Voyeurism, the Look and Dwoskin," *Afterimage* 6 (1976), esp. 44–45.

15. Gayle Rubin, "The Traffic in Women: Notes on the 'Political Economy' of Sex," *Toward an Anthropology of Women*, ed. Rayna Reiter (New York: Monthly Review Press, 1975).

16. On female destinies and the erotic plot, see Nancy Miller, *The Heroine's Text* (New York: Columbia University Press, 1980).

17. Kathleen McLuskie observes of Shakespeare's plays generally that "sex and sexual relations" are "sources of comedy" and "narrative resolution" rather than part of the conflict or the serious business of war and politics. See "The Patriarchal Bard: Feminist Criticism and Shakespeare: *King Lear* and *Measure for Measure*," *Political Shakespeare*, ed. Jonathan Dollimore and Alan Sinfield (Ithaca: Cornell Univ. Press, 1985), 92.

18. Lévi-Strauss, *The Elementary Structures of Kinship*, tr. James Harle Bell, John Richard von Sturmer, and Rodney Needham (Boston: Beacon Press, 1969), 115. For a fuller discusion of *exchange* and feminist theory, see my

"Directing Traffic: Subjects, Objects and the Politics of Exchange," *differences* 2 (1990): 41–54.

19. Julia Kristeva, *Texte du roman* (The Hague: Mouton, 1970), 160.

20. Irigaray, *Ce sexe qui n'en est pas un*, 189, my translation. (See also chap. 3, n. 34 above.)

21. Eve Kosofsky Sedgwick, "Sexualism and the Citizen of the World: Wycherley, Sterne and Male Homosocial Desire," *Critical Inquiry* 11 (1984), 227. See also her *Between Men: English Literature and Male Homosocial Desire* (New York: Columbia University Press, 1985).

22. Michel Serres, "Platonic Dialogue," *Hermes, Literature, Science, Philosophy*, ed. Josue V. Harari and David Bell (Baltimore: Johns Hopkins University Press, 1982), 67.

23. Michel Serres, *Le Parasite* (Paris: Grasset, 1980).

24. Serres's notion of dialogue and the *tiers exclu* in particular helps to make sense of that final moment in *The Elementary Structures of Kinship* when Lévi-Strauss admits women "could never become just a sign and nothing more, since even in a man's world she is still a person, and since in so far as she is defined as a sign she must be recognized as a generator of signs...in contrast to words, which have wholly become signs, woman has remained at once a sign and a value," 496.

25. Walter, xxviii; Herschel Baker, *The Riverside Shakespeare* (Boston: Houghton Mifflin, 1974), 931.

26. Walter, xxviii.

27. Mullaney, *The Place of the Stage*, 87.

28. The "source" of this attribution of influence is M. L. Radoff, "The Influence of French Farce in *Henry V* and *The Merry Wives of Windsor*," *MLN* 48 (1933): 427–35. The cornerstone of his argument is the pun on "con," which turns up in contemporary French farces and "would seem a highly improbable...mere coincidence," 435. He neither cites the farces nor gives evidence they were available in England. More importantly, puns on "con" are ubiquitous. James Bellot's French phrase book, published during the Huguenot immigrations to England, offers several clear correspondences with the phonetic renderings of Katherine's accented English, "dat" for "that," "de" for "the," "den" for "then," "wat" for "what," and "fout" for "foot." *Familiar Dialogues* (London, 1586), unique copy at the Folger Shakespeare Library.

29. An exception is Walter Cohen, in *Drama of a Nation* (Ithaca: Cornell University Press, 1985), who is interested in precisely the problem of the incompleteness of the generic kinds, "romantic comedy" and "national historic

drama." He notes that "the basic fallacy of the history play is to assume that politics is everything and consequently to minimize the impact on national affairs of social relations between the aristocracy and other classes," 220.

30. Dollimore and Sinfield, "History and Ideology," 214.

31. For Bakhtin's formulation of carnival, see *Rabelais and His World,* tr. Hélène Iswolsky (Bloomington: Indiana University Press, 1984); see also *Critical Inquiry* 10 (1983), a forum on Bakhtin. See also Wayne Booth's discussion of Bakhtin's work on Rabelais, "Freedom of Interpretation: Bakhtin and the Challenge of Feminist Criticism," *Critical Inquiry* 9 (1982): 45–76.

32. Jacques Derrida, *Positions,* tr. Alan Bass (Chicago: University of Chicago Press, 1972), 41–42.

<h2 style="text-align:center">CHAPTER 7</h2>

1. On dress in the early modern period, see F. W. Fairholt, *Costume in England: A History of Dress* (London: Chapman and Hall, 1846); Lisa Jardine, *Still Harping on Daughters* (Sussex: Harvester Press, 1983), esp. chap. 5. More generally, see Quentin Bell, *On Human Finery* (London: Hogarth Press, 1976); René Konig, *The Restless Image* (London: Allen and Unwin, 1973); Kaja Silverman, "Fragments of a Fashionable Discourse," *Studies in Entertainment: Critical Approaches to Mass Culture,* ed. Tania Modleski (Bloomington: Indiana University Press, 1986).

2. Though beyond the scope of this chapter, women's alleged preoccupation with dress must be seen in light of clothing as women's primary disposable property.

3. *William Harrison's Description of England,* ed. F. J. Furnivall, *New Shakespeare Society* (1877) Series VI, vol. 1, 168. For other contemporary English attitudes toward dress, see *Early English Poetry, Ballads and Popular Literature of the Middle Ages,* "Satirical Songs and Poems on Costume," ed. F. W. Fairholt (London: Richards, 1849), Vol. XXVII.

4. Ben Jonson, *Every Man Out of His Humour,* I, i.

5. *Phillip Stubbes's Anatomy of the Abuses in England,* ed. F. J. Furnivall, *New Shakespeare Society* (1879) Series VI, no. 6, 31.

6. William B. Rye, *England as Seen by Foreigners* (London: John Russell Smith, 1865), 71.

7. *Stubbes's Anatomy,* 248–49.

8. John Stow, *Annales of England,* continued by Edmund Howes (London, 1632), Dddd1$^{v}$2$^{r}$.

9. Henry Thew Stephenson, *Shakespeare's London* (New York: Henry Holt, 1906), 30.

10. Rye, 263, n. 118.

11. Nicolaas Zwager, *Glimpses of Ben Jonson's London* (Amsterdam: Swets & Zeitlinger, 1926), 125. For additional details of women's dress in early modern England, see *Pleasant Quippes for Upstart Newfangled Gentlewomen*, ed. E. J. Howard (London, 1595; rpt. Oxford, Ohio: Anchor, 1942), thought to be by Stephen Gosson.

12. Joan Thirsk, *Economic Policy and Projects* (Oxford: Clarendon, 1978), 5–6.

13. Martin Holmes, *Elizabethan London* (London: Cassell, 1969).

14. E. K. Chambers, *The Elizabethan Stage* (Oxford: Clarendon, 1923), I, 44, observes that the Queen's "lawndrys" was one of the few paid jobs in her female household.

15. Steve Rappaport, *Worlds within Worlds: Structures of Life in Sixteenth-Century London* (Cambridge: Cambridge University Press, 1989), 13.

16. Printed in Janet Arnold, *Queen Elizabeth's Wardrobe Unlock'd* (Leeds: Maney, 1988), 228. The engraving is of Dutch origin, as was the fashion, practice, and craft of starching neckwear in England. See also Arnold's "Three Examples of Late 16th- and Early 17th-Century Neckwear," *Waffen und Kostumkunde* (Munich, 1973), II, 109–24.

17. Winifrid Hooper, "The Tudor Sumptuary Laws," *English Historical Review* 30 (1915): 435.

18. Quoted in *Stubbes's Anatomy*, I, 244.

19. *A Booke Containing all such Proclamations...*, ed. Humfrey Dyson (London, 1618), 20 Oct. 1559.

20. See, of course, the many how-to books about courtiership. Sumptuary legislation sometimes prohibited not only the wearing of swords by those below the status of knight, it also banned schools of fencing that taught swordsmanship. On social mobility in early modern London, see Rappaport, *Worlds within Worlds*, chpt. 8.

21. I would take issue with Thomas Laqueur's view of the physiological interchangeability of the sexes based on descriptions of the uterus as an inverted penis, and his claim for the eighteenth century as the moment when sexual difference emerged, *Making Sex* (Cambridge: Harvard University Press, 1990). For an important discussion of the role women play in managing the residue of essentialist beliefs, see Elizabeth Weed's introduction to her collection, *Coming To Terms* (New York: Routledge, 1989).

22. Martin Day, *A Monument of Mortality* (London, 1630), A4$^r$.

23. William Prynne, *The Unloveliness of Lovelockes* (London, 1628), A3$^r$.

24. See Silverman, cited above, and Eugénie Lemoine-Luccioni, *La Robe* (Paris: Editions du Seuil, 1983), 147.

25. Naomi Schor, *Reading in Detail* (New York: Methuen, 1987), 19.

26. On masquerade, see Mary Ann Doane's reading of Joan Rivière, "Film and the Masquerade: Theorising the Female Spectator," *Screen* 23 (1982): 81–82 and Tania Modleski, "Femininity as Mas(s)querade: A Feminist Approach to Mass Culture," *High Theory/Low Culture,* ed. Colin MacCabe (New York: St. Martin's Press), 37–52.

27. *A Select Collection of Old English Plays,* ed. Robert Dodsley (1744), 4th ed., ed. W. Carew Hazlitt (London: Reeves and Turner, 1874), IX, 426.

28. Ben Jonson, *Discoveries* (London: Bodley Head, 1923).

29. See Jonathan Goldberg's discussion of Derrida, history, and ideology in "Speculations: *Macbeth* and Source," *Shakespeare Reproduced,* ed. Jean Howard and Marion F. O'Conner (New York: Methuen, 1987), 247.

CHAPTER 8

1. "Zur Kritik der Politischen Okonomie," Karl Marx and Friedrich Engels, *Werke* (Berlin: Dietz Verlag, 1961) XIII,69; thanks to William Crossgrove for advice in translating.

2. Pasquin's *Palinodia* (1619), quoted in Lawrence Stone, "Inigo Jones and the New Exchange," *Archeological Journal* 114 (1957): 120.

3. John Stow, "The Temporal Government of London, The Haberdashers," *A Survey of the cities of London and Westminster* (London, 1755), II, 4A$^v$. Stow's *Survey* appeared in a number of editions in the early seventeenth and eighteenth centuries, each editor adding material from local archives and records. This passage does not appear in the earliest edition but dates the description directly ("within forty years after, about the Year 1580") and by lexical evidence: the *OED* cites late sixteenth- and early seventeenth-century uses of *agglet,* points or tags for threading eylets, but by late in the century the word required definition in glossaries as archaic. Similarly, *frizado,* silk plush, was by the eighteenth century a clear indication of the outdated and old fashioned.

4. Herbert Marcuse, *One Dimensional Man* (Boston: Beacon, 1964); and Stewart Ewen, *Captains of Consciousness* (New York: McGraw-Hill, 1976) develop most forcefully lack or scarcity as a consequence of consumption.

5. For a discussion of consumption as a symbolic activity, see Mary Douglas and Baron Isherwood, *The World of Goods* (New York: Basic, 1979). On the world of goods in early modern Europe, see among others, Lawrence Stone, cited above; Joan Thirsk, *Economic Policy and Projects: The Development of Consumer Society in Early Modern England* (Oxford: Clarendon, 1978); Chandra Mukerji, *From Graven Images: Patterns of Modern Materialism* (New York: Columbia University Press, 1983); and most recently, Simon Schama, *The Embarrassment of Riches: An Interpretation of Dutch Culture* (Cambridge: Harvard University Press, 1987).

6. Jean Baudrillard, *Le système des objets* (Paris: Gallimard, 1968), 98.

7. Karl Marx, *Capital*, I, ii. Quoted in Rachel Bowlby, *Just Looking: Consumer Culture in Dreiser, Gissing and Zola* (London: Methuen, 1985), 27.

8. For discussion of consumption in early modern London, see F. J. Fisher, "The Development of London as a Centre of Conspicuous Consumption in the Sixteenth and Seventeenth Centuries," *Transactions of the Royal Historical Society,* 4th series, 30 (1948): 37–40; also Thirsk and Mukerji, cited above.

9. Heinrich Bullinger, *The Christian State of Matrimony*, tr. Myles Coverdale, (London, 1575), 34$^v$.

10. Thomas Becon, "Catechisme," *Workes* (London, 1564), xx2 $^v$.

11. See chapter 1 above, particularly the quotation from Becon, p. 10.

12. See, for example, Constance Jordan, "Feminism and the Humanists: The Case of Sir Thomas Elyot's *Defence of Good Women*," *Renaissance Quarterly* 35 (1983): 181–201.

13. Though I am looking at woman primarily as consumer, there are numerous examples of women as sellers in the period, from Heywood's *Faire Maide of the Exchange* in which the middle class heroine withstands the blandishments of a higher ranking seducer, to *Tell-Trothes New Yeares Gift* (1593) in which merchants are chastised for marrying "suche matchless paragons as are for neatnesse not to be mated in a countrey" to set them "in their shoppes to tole in customers" with only the proviso that "they keepe them out of their mony boxes and closecubberds" (18).

14. For a general discussion of Jonson's metropolitan topicality that does not address issues of gender, see Leo Salingar, "Farce and Fashion in *The Silent Woman*," *Essays and Studies* 20 (1967): 29–46. Susan Wells argues that Jonson represents a transitional moment when the marketplace is no longer a communal gathering place but simply a location of exchange and profit in "Jacobean City Comedy and the Ideology of the City," *ELH* 48 (1981): 38.

15. Ben Jonson, *Epicoene*, ed. Edward Partridge (New Haven: Yale University Press, 1971). All references are to this edition.

16. Margaret Ezell shows that in the early seventeenth century, women began to participate in such educational associations, in *The Patriarch's Wife* (Chapel Hill: University of North Carolina Press, 1986).

17. Donald Lupton, *London and the Countrey Carbanadoed*, 25–26, quoted by Fran C. Chalfant, *Ben Jonson's London* (Athens: University of Georgia Press, 1978), 72.

18. Jonas Barish observes that though Jonson's presentation of cosmetics is based on Ovid's *Ars amatoria,* Ovid emphasizes the factitious rather than the natural; "Ovid, Juvenal, and *The Silent Woman,*" *PMLA* 71 (1956): 213–24. Whereas in Ovid cosmetics are represented as concoctions of natural ingredients—milk and honey—Jonson's metaphors are taken from metalwork: women are gilders whose finished products are likened to statues and canvases all painted and burnished. On the economics of the *blason,* see Patricia Parker, *Literary Fat Ladies* (London: Methuen, 1987).

19. By the Restoration, Mrs. Otter is no longer remembered for her fortune or her social aspirations but merely as a type of the domineering wife and "Tom Otter" as the henpecked husband. Pepys reports that Charles II said of his brother James that he "would go no more abroad with this Tom Otter and his wife. Tom Killigrew, being by, answered, 'Sir, pray which is the best for a man, to be a Tom Otter to his wife or to his mistress?' meaning the King's being so to Lady Castlemayne"; J. F. Bradley and J. A. Adams, *The Jonson Allusion Book* (New Haven: Yale University Press, 1922), 336.

20. See Norman Brett-James, *The Growth of Stuart London* (London: Allen & Unwin, 1935) and Fisher, cited above. For a discussion of James's urban policy and Jonson's middle masques, see Leah Marcus, "'Present Occasions' and the Shaping of Ben Jonson's Masques," *ELH* 45 (1978): 201–25.

21. Quoted by Fisher, 45.

22. C. H. McIlwain, *The Political Works of James I* (Cambridge: Harvard University Press, 1918), 343–44.

23. John Chamberlain, *The Letters of John Chamberlain,* ed. Norman E. Mc-Clure (Philadelphia: American Philological Society, 1939), II, 475.

24. Richard Ohmann, "Modes of Order," *Linguistics and Literary Style,* ed. Donald C. Freeman (New York: Holt, Rinehart and Winston, 1970), 213, 215.

25. P. M. Handover, *Arbella Stuart* (London: Eyre and Spottiswoode, 1957), 243.

26. Handover, 75.

27. Horatio F. Brown, ed., *Calendar of State Papers and Manuscripts, Venice* (London: Eyre and Spottiswoode, 1900), X, 54.

28. Chamberlain, I, 253.

29. Elizabeth Cooper, *The Life and Letters of Lady Arabella Stuart* (London: Hurst and Blackett, 1866), II, 296–97.

30. Chamberlain, I, 434, 437.

31. *Calendar of State Papers and Manuscripts, Venice*, IX, 42.

32. Lynn Hunt, "History as Gesture," a lecture presented at the English Institute, 1988.


EPILOGUE

1. Louis Althusser et al., *Reading Capital*, tr. Ben Brewster (London: New Left Books, 1970), 18. I am grateful to Ellen Rooney, whose presentation on Althusser at the Pembroke seminar provoked this discussion.

2. Althusser, 24.

# INDEX

Abbot, Robert, Bishop of Salisbury, 18, 23
Adelman, Janet, 61–62
Africanus, Leo, 81, 164n31
Althusser, Louis, 20, 39; and interpellation, 25, 26; and reading, 145–46
Amussen, Susan, 23

Bacon, Francis, 82
Bakhtin, M. M., 100, 108, 167n4
Barber, C. L., 100
Barish, Jonas, 174n18
Baudrillard, Jean, 133, 146
Bean, John, 46
Becon, Thomas, 9, 10–11, 19–20, 134
Behn, Aphra, 88–89
Bellot, James: *Familiar Dialogues*, 169n28
Belsey, Catherine, 67–68
Berger, Harry, 61–62
Best, George, 78–80, 84, 85, 87, 89
Bhabha, Homi, 163–64n28
Bible: 150n1; and Genesis story, 3–4, 18, 25, 79, 148n2; Ephesians, 16; Proverbs, 15; and witches, 159n34
*Blason*, 9, 10, 12, 92, 102, 137, 139; *see also* Body
Bodin, Jean, 82
Body (female): in early anatomies,

3–5; and *blason*, 9, 102, 135; fragmentation of, 10–12, 102, 108; punishment of, 26–31, 40, 60, 87, 101–2, 108; representations of, 3–12, 15–16, 49, 101–3; of a wife, 8–10, 16, 27, 28–30; (male): 3–4, 11
Boorde, Andrew, 112–14
Boose, Linda, 58–59, 149n13, 158–59n27, 166n52
Breast, 53, 58–61; and psychoanalysis, 59–60, 62–63
Bullinger, Heinrich: *The Christian State of Matrimony*, 20–21, 26, 134
Burke, Kenneth, 83
Burton, Robert: *Anatomy of Melancholy*, 111
Butler, Judith, 23

Catholicism, 54, 67, 142
Cavell, Stanley, 70
Cecil, Sir Robert, Earl of Salisbury, 131, 140
Cecil, William, Lord Burghley, 117
Chamberlain, John, 138–39, 141
Clark, Stuart, 157n16
Class, xix, 40, 90–92, 111, 120, 123
Coke, Sir Edward, 68
Cohen, Walter, 169–70n29
Coleridge, Samuel T., 71, 73, 74
Colonialism, xix, 12, 89, 97–99, 137–38, 161n11, 164n31

INDEX

Scarry, Elaine, 148n2
Schor, Naomi, 123
Scot, Reginald: *Discoverie of Witchcraft*, 55–56, 66
Sedgwick, Eve Kosofsky, 105, 163n24
Series (grammatical), 111, 123–24, 139–141
Serres, Michel, 105–6, 169n24
Sexual difference: and binary thought, 18–19, 23–26, 31, 39, 106, 108, 158n26; in early anatomies, 3–5, 11–12; in early modern England, 3–12, 17, 23, 92, 120, 123, 140, 171n21; and essentialism, 120; and "method," 21–25; and voice, 6
Sexuality, 50, 62–63; female, 10–12, 21, 25–26, 92; sexual economies, 86–88, 91–92, 164–65n34
Seymour, William, 142
Shakespeare, William, 58, 92, 146; *Antony and Cleopatra*, 92; and audience, 164n30; and equivocation, 68, 160n41; *Henry V*, 95–108, 167n4, 167–68n8; *Henry VIII*, 111; *King Lear*, 92; *Macbeth*, 53–70, 92; *Othello*, 70–93, 164n34; *The Taming of the Shrew*, 35–50, 155n19; *Titus Andronicus*, 82
Shaw, George Bernard, 139
Shrews, xviii, 27–30, 35–36, 56–57, 143; *see also* Shakespeare: *The Taming of the Shrew;* Skimmingtons
Silverman, Kaja, 122
Skimmingtons, 11, 27–31, 35–36, 39–41, 49; and cowlstaff, 35, 153n1; defined, 27–28
Slavery, 80–83, 89–90, 165n41

Snawsel, Robert: *A Looking Glasse for Married Folkes*, 1, 25
Speckarde, Dorothy, 116
Spivak, Bernard, 85
Spufford, Margaret, 7
Starch, 115, 117–18, 171n16
Stow, John, 143, 146; *Annales of England*, 114–17; *Survey*, 131–32, 140, 172n3
Stuart, Arbella, 140–43
Stubbes, Phillip: *Anatomy of Abuses*, 112, 114, 116–19, 121, 122
Subjectivity (female): construction of, xviii, 7, 18, 26–27, 68–70, 98–104, 143; (male): construction of, xix, 98, 126
Suleiman, Susan, 63–64

Tamar Cam, 99
*Taming of a Shrew, The*, 46, 154n5
*Tell-Trothes New Yeares Gift*, 173n13
Thirsk, Joan, 116–17
Thomas, Keith, 54–56, 159n37
Tilney, Edmund, 27
Travel writing, 78–81, 97–99, 162n17

Underdown, David, xvii, 40–41

Van Meteren, Emanuel, 114, 122
Van Senden, Casper, 81
Vickers, Nancy, 102
Virgil: *Georgics*, 12

Waterhouse, Agnes, 60–61, 66–67, 70, 146
Weed, Elizabeth, 171n21

INDEX

*181*